Robert Greenberg
The Bounds of Freedom: Kant's Causal Theory of Action

Kantstudien-Ergänzungshefte

Im Auftrag der Kant-Gesellschaft
herausgegeben von
Manfred Baum, Bernd Dörflinger
und Heiner F. Klemme

Band 191

Robert Greenberg

The Bounds of Freedom: Kant's Causal Theory of Action

DE GRUYTER

ISBN 978-3-11-061175-5
e-ISBN (PDF) 978-3-11-049412-9
e-ISBN (EPUB) 978-3-11-049184-5
ISSN 0340-6059

Library of Congress Cataloging-in-Publication Data
A CIP catalog record for this book has been applied for at the Library of Congress.

Bibliographic information published by the Deutsche Nationalbibliothek
The Deutsche Nationalbibliothek lists this publication in the Deutsche Nationalbibliografie; detailed bibliographic data are available on the Internet at http://dnb.dnb.de.

© 2018 Walter de Gruyter GmbH, Berlin/Boston
This volume is text- and page-identical with the hardback published in 2016.
Druck und Bindung: Hubert & Co. GmbH & Co. KG, Göttingen

♾ Gedruckt auf säurefreiem Papier
Printed in Germany

www.degruyter.com

In memory of my mother and father

Contents

Acknowledgements —— XI

Preface —— XIII

1 Introduction —— 1
1.1 Controversy Over Kant's Moral Theory —— 1
1.2 Three of Kant's Causal Concepts —— 5
1.3 Single-Object and Dual-Object Ontology —— 7
1.4 Actions and Events —— 8
1.5 Summary of the Scope and Limits of the Book —— 13

2 Causal Theories of Objects and Grice's Causal Theory of Perception —— 14
2.1 Introduction —— 14
2.2 Grice's Basic Idea —— 17
2.3 A Consequence of Grice's Theory —— 19
2.4 A Contrast Between Causation in Perception and Ordinary Causation Based on This Consequence of Grice's Theory, i.e. the Imperceptibility of the Agent —— 21
2.5 A Second Consequence of Grice's Theory —— 24
2.6 Applications of the Second Consequence of Grice's Theory —— 26
2.7 The Logical Connection Between the Two Consequences of Grice's Theory As Applied to All the Examples —— 31
2.8 Explanation of the Connection between the Two Consequences —— 33
2.9 The Two Consequences of Grice's Theory, the Single-object/Dual-Aspect Ontology Involved in the Theory, and Time —— 36
2.10 An Objection to 2.9. and a Reply —— 39

3 Kant's Theory of Practical Causality —— 41
3.1 Transition from Grice to Kant —— 41
3.2 Application of Kant's Causal Theory of Action: Kant's *Incompatibilism* —— 46
3.3 Application of Kant's Non-causal Theory of Action: His *Compatibilism* —— 49
3.4 The Three Alternative Views and the Texts —— 51
3.5 Recent Views About Kant on Rational Agency —— 52
3.6 Rejection of Recent Views —— 54

3.7   Grice's and Kant's Causal Theories and Time —— 55

4   Conscience: Remembering One's Forbidden Actions —— 57
4.1   Another Way to Derive the Timelessness of the Causality of the Freedom of the Will —— 57
4.2   Analysis of the Epigram —— 58

5   The New Problem of the Imputability of Actions —— 61
5.1   The New Problem of the Imputability of Actions —— 61
5.2   The Moral Law is the Practical Causal Law —— 65
5.3   Solutions to the Old Imputability Problem —— 66
5.4   The Solution to the New Imputability Problem —— 70
5.5   Laws of Freedom and Laws of Nature and the Solution to the New Problem of Imputability —— 72
5.6   Hud Hudson's Front-loading —— 74
5.7   The Problem of the Imputability of Actions as a Fundamental Mistake —— 77
5.8   Korsgaard's and My Respective Corrections of the Mistake —— 78
5.9   Conclusion —— 79

6   Maxims and Categorical Imperatives —— 81
6.1   The Possibility of Particular Categorical Imperatives —— 81
6.1.1   Two Apparent Problems with the Conclusion of the Last Chapter —— 81
6.1.2   Maxims can be Categorical Imperatives —— 84
6.2   Maxims, Categorical Imperatives, and a Presumed Omission in Kant's Derivation of the First Formulation of the Categorical Imperative —— 86
6.2.1   A Presumed Omission in Kant's Derivation of the Universalizability Formula of the Categorical Imperative —— 86
6.2.2   Hegel and the Traditional Criticism of the Derivation —— 88
6.2.3   The Validity of the Derivation —— 89
6.2.4   The Origin of the Illusion —— 93
6.2.5   Wood's Rational Egoist Objection —— 97
6.2.6   Conclusion —— 98

7   Necessity and Practical *A Priori* Knowledge: Kant and Kripke —— 99
7.1   The *A Priori* Knowledge and Necessary Truth of Categorical Imperatives —— 99
7.2   Kripke's Complaint About Kant —— 100

7.3	The Target Statement of Kripke's Complaint about Kant —— 101	
7.4	Kant's Shift from Theoretical to Practical Knowledge —— 103	
7.5	The Unsuitability of Happiness as a Universal Principle of Action —— 105	
7.6	The Unsuitability of a Precept as a Practical Law (*praktische Gesetz*) —— 106	
7.7	Subjective Necessity as Both Practical Contingency and Natural Necessity —— 107	
7.8	Practical Laws and Precepts —— 108	
7.9	Kant's Practical Causal Laws as Kripke's Necessities —— 110	

8 The Bounds of Freedom —— 112
8.1   Making Objects Actual —— 112
8.2   The Non-legislative Form of a Maxim Creates a Certain Problem for Our Interpretation of Kant's Moral Law —— 113
8.3   Action without Passion and Independent of Nature —— 114
8.4   The Center of the Circle of Maxims —— 115
8.5   The Last Word: The Incentive to be Moral —— 116

References —— 118

Subject index —— 120

Acknowledgements

Two earlier versions of portions of chapters of this monograph have been read at philosophical conferences, and one of these has been published in a philosophical journal, the other in the proceedings of the conference. An earlier version of much of Chapter 6 of the monograph was read at the American Philosophical Association Meetings, Eastern Division, 2011. I wish to express my thanks to Sidney Axinn for his useful comments on the paper. And I want to thank the editors and publisher of *Kantian Review* for their kind permission to use some of that material for an article that appeared in *KR* in volume 16, 2011. Chapter 5 contains material that was read at the 12th International Kant Congress, Vienna, 2015, and I want to thank the Congress and the publisher of the Proceedings of the Congress, Walter de Gruyter, for permission to use that material here.

I am also indebted to Jeremy Fantl for his helpful comments on 2.4.–5. and to Alan Berger for his useful comments about some of my earlier work on Saul Kripke on necessity, which found its way into 7.

Preface

1 A Personal Note

I am occasionally bothered by historians of philosophy whose impatience with certain evidently objectionable but admittedly important views of a great philosopher lead the historian to attribute the views, obviously not to the admirable side of the philosopher for which the historian says the philosopher is justly renowned, but to an unfortunate legacy that held the philosopher captive and created a blemish on an otherwise deserving eminence in the philosophical world. Since my research revolves primarily around Immanuel Kant, it is commentators on Kant who have especially bothered me in this regard. Of these, Allen W. Wood is particularly noteworthy. His acerbic critique of Kant's theory of transcendental freedom, or noumenal causality, on which Kant says practical freedom, or the freedom of the will, depends, is a case in point.

> Kant is convinced that natural cause explanations require the natural necessitation of an event by preexisting states of the world independently of the adoption of any intention or normative principle by the agent (KpV 5:94–96).[1] If this (incompatibilist) view is correct, then normative law explanations of human actions [such as Wood endorses and adopts in his interpretation of the good side of Kant's ethical thought] cannot be reconciled with natural law explanations at all except through a *desperate expedient* such as Kant's infamous distinction between phenomenal and noumenal causality.[2]

Kant's transcendental idealism has never struck me, however, as a "*desperate expedient*," although in our day and age the transcendental idealistic distinction

---

[1] All references in parentheses in the body of the text are to Kant's works and are to the Akademie edition (Ak) of *Kants gessammelte Schriften* (Berlin: Walter de Gruyter, 1902-, volume and page number) and/or to the *Groundwork of the Metaphysics of Morals* (G), the *Critique of Pure Reason* (KrV), following the standard notation of the A and B pagination of the first and second editions, the *Critique of Practical Reason* (KpV), the *Metaphysics of Morals* (MS), and *Religion Within the Bounds of Mere Reason* (R), (translations either by various translators or myself), except where references are made to the text itself. *Or*, references that are hierarchically Arabic numerated, such as (1.1.) or 2.1., whether within or without parentheses, are references to chapters and sections in the text of the monograph itself. The context also should determine whether the footnote is a reference to Kant's work or to the monograph.
[2] Allen W. Wood, *Kant's Ethical Thought* (Cambridge, UK: Cambridge University Press, 1999), p. 173 (italics added). See also his, "Kant's Compatibilism," in *Self and Nature in Kant's Philosophy*," ed. Allen W. Wood (Ithaca and London: Cornell University Press, 1984), pp. 84–5. See also Jonathan Bennett, "Kant's Theory of Freedom," in *Self and Nature in Kant's Philosophy*," ed. Allen W. Wood (Ithaca and London: Cornell University Press, 1984), pp. 102–12.

which it entails is indeed "infamous." However, rather than pronounce Kant's noumenal causality anathema because of its wholly *a priori* and àtemporal character, I have tried to find a way to understand it more sympathetically or even positively in terms of analytic philosophy. This book is the result of that attempt insofar as Kant's theory of transcendental freedom, or noumenal causality, is, as Kant asserts it to be, the basis of the role of practical freedom, or the freedom of the will, in what I am going to argue is *Kant's causal theory of the origin of an action*.

2 On the Origin of Certain Theses

The causal origin of most of the main theses of the book was hardly a clear analysis of the meaning of the basic terms of Kant's moral theory. As I have said, I have tried to find a way to sympathetically understand perhaps the most difficult term of all, viz., Kant's notion of noumenal causality and its connection with his notion of the freedom of the will, and the book is the product of that effort. The understanding often began with what seemed an insight of what I took to be a truth about one of Kant's terms, but the insight stopped short of revealing the path to its analysis. The course of the evolution from insight to understanding would be of no interest to anyone but myself except perhaps with respect to one particular thesis that has served to structure the book, and though this thesis began, like the others, with an apparent insight, the method with which I tried to analyze the term turned out to be the precisely the obstacle that kept me from finding the analysis that I sought.

It was already clear to me that Kant considered an agent's performance of an action that did not causally depend on certain empirical conditions to consist of a *practical causal relation* between her will and her performance: if, *per contra*, the performance *were* empirically conditional, the causal relation would be natural and not practical. If, say, an agent commits to a certain objective without the caveat that certain empirical conditions obtain, she makes an unconditional commitment to the objective: the commitment is the effect of just her will and not any empirical conditions affecting it. The practical causal connection, Kant maintains, being an instance of efficient causality, entails a causal law between the cause and the effect—between the will and the commitment—which, because the commitment is unconditional, is practical. This answers the question concerning the nature of the law that connects the will and the action, viz., that it is practical and not natural.

I had already decided that the only proposition that was recognized as a law by Kant that could be the causal law that connects the freedom of the will and an action, i.e. the practical causal law, was the moral law, i.e. the Categorical Imperative. Natural law for Kant made the practical causal connection between the will and the action impossible, since natural and practical causal law are for Kant logical contraries.

I reached this conclusion on the following two grounds, both of which are strictly textual. First, Kant introduces the discussion of the causality of the freedom of the will in the Third Section of the *Groundwork* by stating that "the will must be a causality in accordance with immutable laws, but of a special kind" (G 4:446).[3] He continues by saying that the freedom of the will is its "property of being a law to itself" (ibid.). This immediately leads to his assertion that "the proposition, the will in all its actions is a law to itself," designates (*bezeichnet*) the principle, "to act on no other maxim than that which can also have as object itself as a universal law" (G 4:447). The "proposition" Kant is talking about is none other than the *third* formulation of the Categorical Imperative, i.e. the principle of the *autonomy* of the will, and the principle that he says is "designated" by the proposition he is talking about is the *first* formulation of the Categorical Imperative, the principle of the *universalizability* of a maxim of an action. Since these remarks about both formulations of the Categorical Imperative belong to his statement of the causality of "the will in all its actions ..." that introduces the topic of the causality of the will at the beginning of the Third Section of the *Groundwork*, it is undeniable that for Kant the *causality* of the will with respect to its actions logically depends on the *causal law* that connects the will with its actions. Therefore, since the causality of the will involves the causal law and the latter logically depends on the Third and the First formulations of the Categorical Imperative, the causal "immutable laws" of the freedom of the will all conform to these formulations. The Categorical Imperative that is formulated in these formulations can therefore fairly be said to be the *causal* connection itself—the connection that constitutes the causal law—between the freedom of the will and its actions; the Imperative can be said to be the *practical causal law in general* that connects the will and its actions in general.

According to my causal interpretation of the two formulations of the Categorical Imperative that have here been adduced in support of my thesis, they state conditions of a causal connection between the will and an action. In our case, the commitment in question—the action—consists in the unconditional necessity of the rule—the universalizability required by the First formulation of the Categorical Imperative—and the autonomy of the will—the Third formulation of the Imperative—according to both of which the commitment can only be made.

---

[3] More textual evidence for this claim is to be found in the *Critique of Practical Reason*, KpV 5:47, 49.

The will can therefore make the commitment only according to the moral law: the possibility of the commitment consists in the law, and the possibility of the law depends on the freedom of the agent's will.

To sum up, Kant's reasoning seems to be that if the will through its freedom makes the law and the law is the causal connection with an action, and therefore the action is the causal *consequent* of the connection, i.e. the causal conditional, the action is the effect of the freedom of the will. Consequently, the free will produces the action. The properties of autonomy and universality of the Categorical Imperative that explain how the freedom of the will is able to make the causal law and thus the causal connection with the action and therefore produce the action seem very strong grounds in support of my thesis that the Categorical Imperative is the practical causal law between the free will and an action in general. This is one of the main theses of the monograph that follows.

The other ground for the conclusion was Kant's own process of elimination (G 4:446). Since the only alternative to the moral law was a natural law—these being the only kinds of law that Kant says can be known, laws of transcendental freedom being unknowable—and since I believe that Kant is an incompatibilist with respect to the logical relation between the freedom of the will and what I, apparently like most other Kant scholars, take to be his theory of the *determinism* of natural law, only the moral law, whose very possibility for Kant depends on that freedom, has to be, by the very process of elimination that Kant himself employs in this regard, the causal law in question.[4]

The conclusion also fits the lesson Kant said he learned from Hume. Obviously, no necessary connection between logically distinct things can be logically necessary, where logic is understood as Hume meant "logic," Kant meant "general logic," and we mean "formal logic." According to Kant's terminology the connection can be only a synthetic *a priori* proposition or judgment. Since the necessity of a synthetic *a priori* proposition or judgment of interest to Kant—natural and moral—is not logically necessary, the possibility of the necessity requires a condition that is narrower, and in that sense stronger, than logic. For natural necessity, the condition is the transcendental unity of apperception, or objective self-consciousness, and for moral necessity it is the freedom of the will. This freedom is therefore the necessary condition of the possibility of the causal connection between the will and an action, that is, it is the necessary con-

---

[4] But see 1.1. and 1.4. and 3.3. below for my account of Kant's two alternate notions of human action, where only one of which involves his concept of a maxim of an action, and their corresponding involvement of natural causal law.

dition of the possibility of the moral law's being the practical causal law that connects the will and an action.

Despite all of Kant's talk about the moral law's being an imperative—a statement about, following Hume's famous formulation, what *ought* to be in contrast to what *is*, I was still expecting a statement of a causal law to be in either the *indicative* or the *subjunctive* mood, in an expression like "If X occurred, so *would* Y," where the use of the subjunctive expression "would" expresses a causal connection.[5] I failed to see that looking for causal language in Kant's formulations of the Categorical Imperative was precisely the wrong way to go about demonstrating the connection between the concept of cause and effect and the Imperative, and therefore the wrong way of demonstrating the causal connection between the will and an action that I was looking for. As so often happens, at least with me, when pursuing a false lead, it suddenly seemed to dawn on me that instead of looking for causal language in the Categorical Imperative I should begin with Kant's *moral theory* and look for the causal nature of the Categorical Imperative there. That is, I should *begin* with the thesis that the basic elements of his moral theory are to be ordered causally. Simply put, since the basic elements of his moral theory are ordered according to the Categorical Imperative, and since I was adopting a causal approach to Kant's moral theory, their order according to the Imperative should be understood causally. Immediately, and thus independently of what I otherwise consider the persuasive textual arguments given just above, the Imperative becomes the causal law that connects the elements of his moral theory, again, as Kant himself stated they should be in the passage quoted above, despite the fact that the law is expressed in the imperative mood instead of in the indicative or the subjunctive mood as I had expected it to be. Once I reversed the priorities, I applied them to the Categorical Imperative, in particular to its universalizability and autonomy formulations, and the application seemed to hold. Subsequent chapters in the book which attempt to explain Kant's notion of practical causality are arguments in support of this last claim, viz., that the application seemed to hold—arguments in supplementation to the textual arguments already given.

Viewing the order of Kant's moral theory as causal and therefore identifying the order of the terms in the formulations of the Categorical Imperative as causal instead of looking for causal language in the formulations themselves, suggests another reversal of order, this one in the causal order between the terms of nat-

---

[5] Henry E. Allison expresses the same discomfort as I initially felt trying to strictly construe Kant's moral law as a causal law. *Kant's Theory of Freedom* (Cambridge, UK,/New York: Cambridge University Press, 1990), p 244. Whereas Allison gave up on the strict construal, I argue for it in the monograph.

ural causality and those of practical causality. What comes first in a *natural* causal law is what comes first in the causal order of *time*, viz., empirical conditions on the will, which sometimes get translated in Kant's texts as "pathological" conditions, or what Kant considers "external" or "contingent" causal determinations of the will, and their effect is an action that constitutes an *event*—something that happens in what Kant calls the *objective succession of time*. This is *not* an action that Kant ascribes to the will with its property of freedom, and thus is subject to moral judgment. The synthetic *a priori* judgment that causally connects empirical conditions and an action that is independent of moral judgment is Kant's principle of *objective succession* that is stated in his Second Analogy of Experience (KrV A189/B 232ff.). However, according to the method I am following, it is the Categorical Imperative that determines the causal order of Kant's *moral* theory. It is the will that now comes first, and its effect is an action, such that it is an action of the will, the maxim of which consists of the same empirical conditions that come first in the causal order of *time*. Where the natural causal order is temporal, the moral causal order is àtemporal. Where the will is empirically conditioned in the causal order of time, it is empirically unconditioned in the causal order of morality, and the empirical conditions that affect the will in the causal order of time and bring about action are, in the àtemporal causal order of morality, the *effects* of the very same will. The will and empirical conditions reverse their relative causal roles—cause and effect—depending on whether the causal order is natural, and hence temporal, or moral, and hence àtemporal. Thus, an identical object, that is, the subject and its involvement in causal relations, viz., the will—is to be viewed both ways—naturalistically and morally, temporally and àtemporally. For those familiar with the two ways of interpreting Kant's transcendental idealism—dual-aspect versus dual-object view—what I have just said will be recognized as an embrace of the dual-aspect view of the idealism. It is the identical will that is to be viewed as active in the bringing about of a human action and as passive in the course of antecedent empirical conditions that also bring about human action from a naturalistic point of view. In this manner, a more sympathetic or even positive evaluation of Kant's notion of the àtemporal causality of the freedom of the will might have a better chance of success than it has received so far from Kant scholars who come to his theory of free will with a distinctly empiricist philosophical sensibility.

This causal interpretation of the order of Kant's moral theory creates a certain problem, however, a solution to which is proposed later in the book, viz., in 5. The problem is that since the causal law that connects the will and an action is the moral law, it can be asked how it is possible that an action can be immoral. This is the familiar problem in Kant's moral theory known as the issue of the imputability of *immoral* actions to agents whose free will is a necessary condition of the very possibility of morality.[6] Since free will is such a condition, how can immoral actions be imputed to it? Such has been the statement of the problem as viewed from the standpoint of the *justification* of the principles on which one acts, viz., one's maxims, and therefore a concern with the *justification* of one's actions, and thus the *validity* of one's practical reasoning, where the reasoning begins with the practical proposition whose rationality Kant considers self-evident, viz., the Categorical Imperative, and goes on to consider validating the agent's maxims, depending on whether or not they conform to the Imperative. The problem of imputation of immoral actions from this standpoint is, how can the moral law that alone can *justify* a maxim depend on the very freedom of the will to which an immoral action can be imputed. How can an identical property of the will—its freedom—be both necessary for the very possibility of morality and also the subject of an ascription of an immoral action to the same will with that same freedom?

In terms of my causal approach to Kant's moral theory, however, the quest is not *justification* of an agent's maxims, but rather *clarity* among the basic elements of Kant's moral theory, where it is hoped that their causal order will afford us perspicuity regarding their meaning. The question of the imputability of immoral actions to free agents thus becomes instead: how can an identical property of the will—its freedom—be *both* necessary for the very possibility of a causal connection of the will with an action, i.e. the practical causal law, *and* also the causal origin of an action that *violates* the causal law? As indicated, the solution to this problem within my causal approach to Kant's moral theory will be offered later in the book.

Returning to the general causal approach the book takes to Kant's moral theory, the causal approach not only resolved of an important difficulty that I confronted in my work on Kant's theory, but it fit perfectly with a decision that I had made prior to adopting the approach, viz., the decision that I would use a certain causal theory of perception proposed in analytic philosophy as a template for my analysis of Kant's causal theory of action. In both cases, the interpretation of the Categorical Imperative as the causal law connecting the will and an action and the interpretation of the logical connection between a perception and its object as including a causal connection between the object and its perception, the order of the elements involved, whether in the realm of moral theory or in the theory of knowledge of objects, is the concept of cause and effect.

---

[6] See, for example, Hud Hudson, *Kant's Compatibilism*. (Ithaca and London: Cornell University Press, 1994), pp. 157 ff., and Christine Korsgaard *Creating the King*dom of Ends (Cambridge, UK: Cambridge University Press, 1996), pp. 159 ff.

Before closing these remarks about the origins of the main theses of the book, a certain controversy surrounding Kant's causal theory of action should be mentioned again and will be resumed at the beginning of the chapter that follows, viz., the Introduction. It concerns the issue already introduced as the question of whether causal order for Kant must be interpreted as an order of time. The position I have maintained thus far and maintain throughout the book is that time is not only *not* necessary for efficient causal law in the matter of Kant's moral theory and, moreover, makes Kant's treatment of morality incoherent, but also its predominance in our thought about causality generally undermines the chances of the success of a more sympathetic or even positive assessment of Kant's notion of the àtemporal causality of the freedom of the will.

3 An Empirical Analogy with the Freedom of the Will

Perhaps the most inefficient aspect of using a computer for word processing is trying to troubleshoot difficulties on one's own. The user's guide always tells us to check the power cord first, make sure it is firmly inserted in the computer and in the wall socket, and if that does not work, to reboot the computer, and other simple things like that. When the computer starts working again, we are not just relieved that there is nothing wrong with the computer, but we also know that we are incurring the cost of the electricity. Saving on the former is offset a bit by the cost of latter. The computer and the electrical power have traded places in the cause and effect relation: the computer now puts the electrical power to use to perform the word processing.

Kant's reversal of the roles of cause and effect alternately occupied by the two distinct efficient causes of action—free will and the empirical conditions that precede it, but now only in the order of time—is analogous to this advice on how to troubleshoot difficulties with a computer, or with the hundreds of other devices of everyday use. Just as a computer's own word processing power is independent of the electrical current from a wall socket, so the will's power to enact the agent's maxim in the action that ensues is independent of everything except the will and its freedom. Its freedom is essential if it is to produce an action, and therefore it is essential to the agent's moral responsibility. Just as electrical power neither enables nor disables or prevents the computer's own power to process words, so empirical conditions such as an agent's society, culture, and psychology neither enable nor disable or prevent her will to produce an action, that is, its power to enact her maxims, and they therefore cannot affect her moral responsibility for her actions. It is as specious to suppose otherwise as it would be to mistakenly blame a computer's failure to produce some output on a problem with the electricity, if the computer is to blame. But it would be just as specious to blame the will for an agent's aberrant or deviant behavior, if the behavior were due to society, culture, or psychology—as specious as it would be to mistakenly blame a computer's failure to process words on a problem with the computer, if the failure to insert the power cord in the computer or in the wall socket were at fault.

The fallacy of crediting or blaming an external condition for an internal or constitutional condition and vice-versa, crediting or blaming an internal condition for an external one, can in certain circumstances be due to the ease with which we can slide from one efficient causal attribution to the other, neither of which has anything *causal* to do with the other. Yet, and here are the conditional statements that might prompt sliding from one causal attribution to the other, we could truthfully and properly say, *both* "If the *supply of electricity* had failed, the computer would not have resulted in the word processing," and "If the *computer* had failed, the supply of electricity would not have resulted in the word processing." We have thus reached the apparent paradox that the *supply of electricity* would be *both* a cause of the word processing *and* an effect of the *computer*, since if the computer processes words, the supply of electricity would be a necessary ascription of the *processing*—it would be *electrical*. The corresponding apparent paradox is that the *computer* would be *both* a cause of the word processing *and* an effect of the *supply of the electricity*, since the computer, too, would be part of the processing: if the supply of electricity results in word processing, the computer would be a necessary ascription of the processing—it would be *computed*. Analogously, we could truthfully and properly say, "The agent's free will realizes or enacts her maxims through producing her actions," as well as "Were it not for certain social, cultural, or psychological conditions, she would not have produced her actions."

The analogy with the computer and its output both suggests and blocks the agent's moral responsibility for her actions. Her will that produces her actions cannot be affected by her social, cultural, and psychological conditions, and hence she is morally responsible for her actions that are produced by her will, whereas her will is also merely the means by which the same empirical conditions produce the very same actions for which she *cannot* be morally responsible. This is as ordinary a distinction as we find in our everyday experience. It is why Kant could point to everyone's common sense as evidence for the presence of morality, and thus of the freedom of the will in all of us, and seems as far from a *"desperate expedient"* as it seems a notion might be, despite the paradoxical fact that empirical conditions have caused people to do what they do. Of course, the empirical distinction between a computer and electricity with respect to output does not contain the *a priori* complications that belong to the relation between the freedom of the will and action, and conversely. But the computer and the supply of electricity indicate that Kant's notion of the freedom of the will as noumenal causality can be approached by analogy with empirical distinctions that we readily make everyday of our lives—the distinction between our will that *a priori* is causally responsible for our actions, on the one hand, and the empirical conditions that *a posteriori* are causally responsible for our actions, now naturalistically considered, on the other hand. It is Kant's distinction between the *a priori* property of the will that is its freedom and the receptivity of the will to *empirical* conditioning that is the basis of his twofold claim that only free will can make an agent morally responsible for her actions and yet her actions are completely determined by antecedent empirical conditions according to natural laws.

With that, we enter into an attempt to get clarity on this *a priori* property of the will, viz., its freedom, that is at once so familiar and yet so difficult to understand in terms of the philosophy that reigns today in the empiricist naturalistically oriented Anglophone Kantian circles of analytic philosophy. The introduction to the solution begins in the next chapter.

1 Introduction

1.1 Controversy Over Kant's Moral Theory

Controversy embroils Kant's moral theory with respect to two, reciprocal conditions. On the one hand, his formulas for determining the morality of an action are alleged to be so abstract, given their pretense to be not just *a priori*, but purely rational, that they allow every conceivable action and therefore demand none. That is, they are devoid of the content that moral theory requires if it is to determine any specific action. Combined under the title of Categorical Imperative, which Kant also calls the moral law, the formulas leave his moral theory empty of substance or content. Better to look to *experience*, it is alleged, to provide the sought for specifications of action: experience that includes what Kant himself agrees are our humanly unavoidable inclinations, desires, passions, and various other motivations. Kant's claim that *pure* practical reason to be a source, or "determining ground," of the will and therefore possibly of certain of its actions is his fundamental mistake in seeking the "groundwork" of the possibility of a moral judgment of an action. Applying reason to the actual empirical facts about our moral thought is the only possible guide to engaging in philosophical discussion of moral theory, it is contested by Kant's critics. Only the empirical application of practical reason carries the genuine promise of being capable of being fulfilled, they contend.

The condition that stands in the reciprocal relation to the pure rationality of the Categorical Imperative is the peculiar nature of the causality of the will that is responsible for action that is subject to moral judgment, the causality we have already discussed in the Preface. The means by which such causality can be represented is the freedom of the will—the causality of the will that is independent of the very empirical facts that *pure*, practical reason must block if it is to be the determining ground of the will. *Pure* for Kant is the *non-empirical*, or non-sensational, character of a representation, where in practical matters for Kant sensations ultimately devolve onto *pleasure* and *pain*. This independence of the causality of the will from these empirical factors is precisely the reciprocity that obtains between the two conditions that fuel the controversy in question—the rationality of the pure moral law and the àtemporal causality of the freedom of the will.

The reciprocal condition of free will is beset with a problem of its own, however. Contrary to Kant's own what his critics consider respectable empiricist analysis of *natural causality* that is found in the Second Analogy of Experience in the *Critique of Pure Reason*, where temporal empirical antecedents are said to be causally responsible for temporal empirical consequents according to natural law, by contrast, only the will that stands outside of time and sensation can be the causal origin of an action that can be brought about and judged according to the moral law, since only an àtemporal causality of the will can be independent of the factors that would otherwise turn Kant's *pure* practical reason into *empirical* practical reason. Thus would the natural causality of the Second Analogy make it impossible for Kant to promulgate the Categorical Imperative as definitive of the moral law. Yet it is his very departure from his admittedly respectable empiricist analysis of causality in the Second Analogy that casts his moral theory into disrepute. For in principle his theory of *pure a priori* non-natural causality—the causality of freedom, whether of the will in practical matters or of things in themselves in theoretical concerns—puts such a strain on our philosophical credulity that we are forced either to turn away from his moral theory altogether or else side-step this odious feature of the causality of free will—its àtemporality—and reconstruct what Kant should have meant in terms that are more congenial to our contemporary empiricist philosophical sensibility.

The work that follows is an essay on Kant's *metaethics*, not his *normative* ethics[1]: it explores what, following W. V. Quine in the quite different context of empirical knowledge,[2] can be called the "meaning" it is claimed Kant attaches to certain key terms in his ethics, such as the freedom of the will and its role in the causal origin of action, in contrast to the validity of a moral judgment about the action or the moral justification of the action in his normative ethics, which, again following Quine, we can assign, according to Quine's distinction, to theory of justification of a reference to an object or a claim to truth.[3] It is therefore primarily concerned with the second of these two reciprocal conditions, viz., the freedom of the will, and so it bypasses the labyrinth of discussions surrounding the great and intricate details of the grounds, or justifications, and consequences of the Categorical Imperative that belong to his moral thought. Its approach to the issue of the philosophical valuation of the àtemporality of Kant's theory of that type of causality, however, will adopt neither of the paths outlined just above that have been followed by previous commentators on this subject; it will neither abjure his moral theory altogether nor will it reconstruct a theory of causality that Kant should have adopted and that would be more in line with his theory of natural causality. Indeed, the discussion that follows will

---

[1] The monograph usually uses "moral" rather then "ethical" to characterize the subject at hand, but not always, since sometimes philosophers would find "ethical" more in tune to current practice. No philosophical point is intended by the preference for "moral."
[2] W. V. O. Quine, "Epistemology Naturalized," in *Ontological Relativity and Other Essays* (New York, NY: Columbia University Press, 1969).
[3] Quine, "Epistemology Naturalized," pp. 71–73.

not begin with his theory of the freedom of the will at all, and thus it will not begin with either of the two reciprocal conditions that have fueled the controversy in question. It will instead begin closer to the *terminus* of his metaethical argument and embark on an analysis of his theory of *action*, in particular, what I consider his *causal* theory of action, and it will proceed to *derive* the àtemporality of the causality of the will from the causal theory. This procedure is in line with that already outlined in the Preface to the book. Rather than begin with his difficult notion of free will, it will instead *end* with it, trusting that the preceding analysis of his concept of action will throw positive light on its nature. Any success such an analysis will have should enhance any correlative positive understanding of the other reciprocal condition, i.e. the rationality of the àtemporal pure will. To sum up, not only will pure rationality *follow* our discussion of free will, but free will itself will depend on the completion of our analysis of Kant's concept of action. Thus will Kant's theory of the freedom of the will turn on his understanding of human action, rather than conversely, which is how most of Kant interpretation seems to have proceeded recently.

An important terminological note: As will be further explained in 1.4. below, Kant uses the term "action" (*"Handlung"*) in a variety of ways, their common feature being that the will is involved, either as the subject to which an action is *ascribed* or as playing a role in the *causal* origin of an action, *or both*. All and only uses that involve *both* ascription of an action to the will *and* the will's causal efficacy with respect to an action's existence are uses that conform to his causal theory of action, as I am interpreting that theory. I consider his use of the term according to his causal theory of action the *primary sense* in which he uses it and that will be the sense that attaches to the term if it appears by itself in the text of the book, that is, appears without further elaboration, which will be clarified in 1.4. below.

Finally, an additional novelty of the approach adopted here is that the discussion of Kant's metaethics begins not only *not* with Kant's theory of the freedom of the will, but not even with his theory of action. Instead it begins with what seems is generally agreed an allied "meta" theory in epistemology (what would be covered by what can fairly be called Kant's *transcendental* epistemology), viz., theory of perception, and, a further limitation, to add to those already mentioned, it does not even begin with perception theory generally, but with a particular theory of perception advanced a while ago by the Oxford analytic philosopher, H. P. Grice.[4] Grice argued that our concept of a perception of a material

---

4 H. P. Grice, "The Causal Theory of Perception," in *Proceedings of the Aristotelian Society*, Supplement, vol. XXXV, 1961, reprinted in large part in *Knowledge: readings in contemporary epistemology*, ed. Sven Bernecker and Fred Dretske (Oxford: Oxford University Press, 2006), pp. 442–451.

object requires that the object play a role in the causal origin of the perception—a not too widely held view among analytic philosophers at the time, but now definitely more popular among them, especially among those who hold a more general causal theory of knowledge. Accordingly, Grice dubbed his contribution to the literature "a *causal* theory of perception." My work on Kant's causal theory of action is an adaptation of Grice's *causal* theory of perception. In this way I hope to accommodate Kant to our current sensitivities to such an inimical idea as pure àtemporal causality. Given the *intelligibility* of Grice's causal theory of perception—a proper subject-matter of epistemology—we should, I think, have a better chance of finding Kant's theory of free action more intelligible as well, including the àtemporal purity of its causal origin— the freedom of the will. Despite analytic philosophy's blanket rejection of Kant's transcendental idealism, it is hoped that the adaptation of Kant to Grice improves the chances of finding greater intelligibility of Kant's theory of free action among analytic philosophers and thus a more sympathetic view of his causal theory of action among them, and thus also his theory of the freedom of the will, and finally, by extension, his normative ethics.

In summary, this book is an attempt to make Kant's concepts of the freedom of the will and its for many Kant scholars notorious atemporal causality intelligible in light of the analytic world's acknowledgement of the intelligibility of Grice's (and Strawson's subsequent) theory of the causality of the perceived object with respect to its own perception. It thus is an essay on the freedom and àtemporal causality of *either* the independent object *or* the will of the subject of the corresponding causal theory of *either* a *perception* or more generally *knowledge* of the object *or action* of the will of the subject, whether in theory of knowledge *or* in theory of action, respectively. It is therefore not the ordinary work of a Kant scholar in Kantian exegesis, consisting of a very close reading of Kantian text or a survey of the secondary literature. It is rather an essay in metaphysics/epistemology that attempts to interpret Kant's freedom of the will and its àtemporal causality on the basis of an analysis of Grice's causal theory of perception—an interpretation of Kant's causal theory of action as an *adaptation* of Grice's causal theory of perception. It thus does not fall within customary studies in either metaphysics and epistemology or in Kant scholarship, which combs through varieties of interpretations of Kantian texts and the secondary literature. Kant scholars looking for the latter may be disappointed in what follows. On the positive side, however, it offers to these same scholars a radically new and I think revealing way of viewing the Categorical Imperative and its implications for Kant's theory of action, viz., as Kant's statement of the *causal* connection he says must exist between an agent and her action, if the maxim of her action and her will are to be subject to moral judgment, instead of as merely a formula for the *justifica-*

tion of an action (or lack thereof)—as it seems to be universally viewed at the present time. Finally, it offers to philosophers generally a statement of some perhaps surprising consequences of Grice's and Strawson's respective causal theories of perception, which therefore are themselves perhaps surprising consequences for causal theories of knowledge in general.

1.2 Three of Kant's Causal Concepts

Adapting its interpretation of Kant's causal theory of action to Grice's causal theory of perception, this study interprets Kant's concept of the freedom of the will as a consequence of his concept of action, where the latter is viewed as a concept of a certain type. Again, the concept-type also applies to Kant's concepts of *appearance* and *event*. By providing a concept-type that subsumes all three concepts— *appearance*, *event*, and *action*—the type can arrange the concepts in a pattern that can improve our understanding of all three, and thereby, for our specific purpose, improve our understanding of Kant's concept of freedom.

Limited though it is to the logical relations of just certain concepts in Kant's philosophical system, this method of understanding his freedom of the will is nonetheless the primary objective of my book. As already indicated, its limitation is especially noteworthy with respect to its stopping short of entering into the myriad controversies surrounding his normative moral theory. Hence, to repeat, it is *not* a book on his normative moral theory. Nor does it enter into the particular details of the meta-theoretical debate Kant is having with empiricism regarding the question of whether the causality of the will should be understood independently of any empirical conditions of the existence of a person's will, details such as a person's upbringing, the culture and society to which she belongs, or her psychological makeup. The reason for its not entering the fray regarding the details of the debate is that empiricists could just as well take exception to my *interpretation* of Kant's theory as it takes exception to the *pure* character of the theory itself, viz., that the will has the property of being free from all empirical conditions in which it actually exists, and therefore a freedom that is completely imperceptible, for my interpretation also takes the freedom to be as pure, and hence as imperceptible, as Kant takes it to be. Consequently, the interpretation is also *not* a defense of the particulars of Kant's argument against empiricists.

As I have already said, however, it is rather an attempt to engender a *positive evaluation* of Kant's notion of the freedom of the will by viewing it as a consequence of his concept of action by bringing *action* under the same concept-type that applies specifically to *appearance* and to *event*, thereby giving us a new way of understanding not only all three concepts together, but more pertinently to our objective, a new way of understanding the concept of freedom by viewing it in its place in this arrangement of these concepts.

The concept-type I am talking about is Kant's use of what is customarily called a "causal theory" of an object. To state it without the precision that it will receive in the next chapter, a causal theory of an object states that the concept of the object logically requires the existence of an independent object as playing a role in the causal origin of the object so conceived. For example, a brief way of describing a causal theory of perception is that the concept of a perception of an independent object logically requires the existence of the independent object as playing a role in the causal origin of the perception of the object. So, the theory of the object *conceived*, e.g. a *perception* of an independent object, is actually an analysis of its concept, e.g., the concept of a perception of an independent object, where the analysis contains the idea that the existence of the independent object plays a role in the causal origin of the *conceived* object, e.g. the perception of the independent object.

My interpretation of Kant's concept of the freedom of the will is, as already noted in the previous section, that it is a *consequence* of Kant's *causal theory of action*. According to the theory, determinations of the will are comprised as an action only if the will is logically required to play a role in the origin of their existence, the action; only then can they be determinations of an action. The argument that the will must be *free* according to this causal theory of action is, in part, that in bringing about an action—an enactment of the principle, or maxim, of the action—the will is *empirically unconditioned*. Otherwise, its ability to bring about the action *would* involve the condition(s). But, to be clear, the proposition that it is empirically conditioned in the way supposedly required for the action, i.e. that the will is the faculty of mind that is so conditioned, is *not* logically implied by the causal theory of action here being ascribed to Kant (and which henceforth will simply be described as "Kant's theory," meaning that this is the primary theory—i.e. the theory without further qualification—my interpretation ascribes to him). Since it *is* logically implied by the proposition that the empirical condition(s) plays a role in the causal origin of the action brought about by the will, that proposition cannot be part of what I mean by "Kant's causal theory of action."

The exclusion of empirical conditions as *causal* determinations of an action from Kant's causal theory of action raises the obvious question introduced in the Preface of the book, viz., the question of the nature of the causal law that connects a person's will and her action. Causal laws are generally supposed to apply to empirical objects; yet being empirically unconditioned, the will is not an empirical object. The answer to be proposed, again as stated in the Preface, is that the practical *causal* law for Kant is none other than the Categorical Imperative, that is, the moral law. To repeat, it will be argued that the moral law is related to the will as its *causal* connection to an action.

In the course of the extended argument to be filled out in the chapters that follow, the concept of an action understood according to Kant's causal theory of action is shown to include the concept of a Kantian appearance, and the concept of the free will that brings about the action according to the moral law is shown to share with the concept of a *thing in itself* the feature that it cannot be *empirically* represented independently of its correlative effect—the appearance in the case of a thing in itself and the action in the case of a free will. Also in the course of the arguments that follow it is shown that for Kant the concept of something that happens according to *natural* law—an *event*—must also be understood according to Kant's *causal* way of understanding a concept introduced at the beginning of this section. Kant can therefore be said to have a causal theory of something's being an event, which means that the concept of an event logically requires the existence of an object that plays a role in its causal origin. But this use of his general causal theory obviously must be distinguished from his use of the theory with regard to an action that is subject to moral judgment, and in the next two sections I state the difference on which the distinction is based.

1.3 Single-Object and Dual-Object Ontology

The present book is of a piece with my previous work on Kant's metatheories,[5] or what, following Quine, we can call his theories of meaning (which Quine also calls "conceptual") as distinct from his normative theories of justification of reference or truth (which Quine also calls "doctrinal"). I have there argued for the so-called single-object/dual-aspect interpretation of Kant's transcendental idealism, in contrast to the dual-object interpretation of the idealism, the same position I have taken in the Preface to this book. As stated there, this is a response to the question of whether the distinction between an appearance and the thing in itself is a distinction between merely two aspects of an identical object or is instead a distinction between two objects which do not span or are not components of the same object. I have opted for the former alternative, and I still do. My arguments for my choice are spelled out in my previous work. The general issue of single-object versus dual-object ontology belongs to metatheory in gen-

---

[5] Robert Greenberg, *Kant's Theory of A Priori Knowledge* (University Park, PA: Penn State Press, 2001), Parts I and II, and *Real Existence, Ideal Necessity: Kant's Compromise* (Berlin and New York: Walter de Gruyter, 2008), Chapters 1–5.

eral, and a single-object ontology need not be Kantian. For example, reverting to Quine again, he holds that it is the *stimulation* that alone can provide the empirical objectivity of what he calls a "radical" translation from a suitably prompted utterance of an expression in a native speaker's radically distinct language ("*Gavagai*") to an expression in a linguist's, or translator's, language ("*rabbit*") —the objectivity of the sole empirical *meaning* of "*Gavagai*."[6] The stimulation is both the meaning of the expressions and the causal origin of the meaning— it is both what is meant and the causal origin of its being so. On a dual-object theory of translation, however, no object comprises the two items, i.e. the meaning and its causal origin. Hence, a translation of an utterance of an expression in the native speaker's language would not be a translation of its stimulation. To sum up, this interpretive issue of single-object versus dual-object ontology arises again in the present work, and as I said, I again choose the former over the latter as the camp to which I belong as I turn my attention to interpretation of Kant's causal theory of action.

1.4 Actions and Events

Although I have said above that Kant's concepts of appearance, event, and action are all concepts of the type according to which a conceived object—an appearance, an event, and an action—causally depends on an independent object, I have also said that I would distinguish between *event* and *action*. In this regard, though an event is an appearance for Kant, not every appearance is an event. Actions, on Kant's causal theory of action, for one, are appearances that are not events.

Actions, on Kant's causal theory, and appearances—the latter specifically in their very introduction into Kant's discussion—are distinguished from events according to a distinction between Kant's two conceptions of causality—a distinction that I find basic to his thought about all of the issues already mentioned in the previous sections. *The distinction, most importantly for our present purposes, divides causal theories of objects into two subtypes of causal theory.* Objects are efficacious because either they are self-sufficient to be so or they are not, i.e. where their causality depends on that of another object. Causality can thus be considered as either internal to the objects themselves—constitutive of their identity—or external to the objects. The causality, or power, of the motion of Hume's billiard ball to move another billiard ball depends on the motion of

---

[6] W. V. O. Quine, *Word and Object* (Cambridge, Mass, New York and London: MIT Press and John Wiley & Sons, Inc., 1960), pp. 30 ff.

yet another object to move the first one—the force of the previous motion is imparted to the object whose causality brings about the motion in question. This would fall under Kant's concept of an event: events causally depend on preceding events if they themselves are to result in subsequent events. The reason that an analysis of such a concept of event qualifies as a causal theory as I employ the notion is that the causality belonging to the power of an external object is included in Kant's concept of an event. That is, the causal dependence of an event on another event is included in the logical, or conceptual, connection between an event and an independent event.

But the causal dependence on an external object is precisely what distinguishes an event from an action and an appearance—again, an appearance in its first occurrence in Kant's discussion. A consequence of the externality of an event is that the logical connection between one event and a preceding event does not include the *specification* or the *definite identification* of the preceding event. The externality entails something that may be said of the preceding event, viz., that it is not *given*, in contrast to its being instead only *thought* through a concept. The logical connection between the concept and the existence of an independent object leaves it to experience or perception to specify or definitely identify the preceding event that otherwise would only remain an object of mere thought. As Strawson aptly puts the general distinction between his and Grice's causal theory of perception, on the one hand, and ordinary or physical causations, on the other hand, the preceding event (in an ordinary or physical causation) is not a *certain* object, or as is more generally said, it is not a *given* object, that is logically required by the subsequent event; rather, it is determined only more generally than would be necessary for a definite identification, that is, for it to be given—determined, therefore, only through a *concept* (in a predicative position in a judgment), and hence can be *definitely* identified or given only through *experience* or *perception* (ultimately requiring an *intuitive*, *indexical*, or *demonstrative* representation).[7] Thus, the externality of the preceding event consists at least in the absence from the concept of the subsequent event, i.e. the effect, say, the concept of (the occurrence of) smoke, the specification of a *certain*, or *given*, object, say, a fire, that plays a role in the causal origin of the subsequent event, the smoke, which, of course, is given. Again, only experience or perception can provide a specification or definite identification of the preceding event.

---

7 P. F. Strawson, "Perception and Its Objects," reprinted in *Knowledge:* readings in contemporary epistemology, ed. Bernecker and Dretske, p. 461. For the distinction between mere identification and definite identification see P. F. Strawson, *Individuals: An Essay in Descriptive Metaphysics* (Methuen & Co. Ltd., 1959), Chapter 1, section 1.

The absence of this specification or definite identification, or, to put it positively, presence of this *generality*, or *conceptualization*, of reference, is missing from the concept of an action or an appearance—at least in the first occurrence of the concept of an appearance in Kant's discussion. The independent object that is causally responsible for an action or for such an appearance is a *certain* object—it is already specified as *the will* of the agent of the action—that has performed the action, or in the case of the causal relation between a thing in itself and an appearance for Kant, it is the *intuited* object that in affecting the mind in a certain way brings about its appearance in the mind (KrV A 19/B 33), or following Grice and Strawson, in the case of the causal relation between a material object and a perception, it is the *perceived* object that plays a role in the causal origin of its perception. With respect to Grice and Strawson, however, there is a fundamental divergence of opinion. Where Grice tried to *further* specify the object in terms of its mode of causal efficacy with respect to its perception, an attempt that got stymied by its circularity, Strawson succeeded in specifying it, and he did so independently of any such mode of causal efficacy as stipulated by Grice, and therefore without the circularity that attended Grice's attempted solution at specification of the object.

Continuing with Strawson's own further examples of the subtype of causal theory according to which the existence of the independent object is *sufficient* in playing its logically required role in the causal origin of its effect, in the sense that it does not causally depend on another object to do so, in Strawson's reference to the causal theory of memory, it is the *remembered* object or event; in a causal theory of a written history of an event, the independent object is specified in the name or description of the *subject* of the history, e. g., the decline and fall of Rome, of Edward Gibbon's history, the subject that causally gives rise to, and thus is causally connected to, the historian's writing about it. Saul Kripke's historical-causal theory of direct reference transmission from the naming of a *given* object, namely, Aristotle, to a later use of his name specifies Aristotle as the historical-causal origin of the later direct reference to him through the use of his name and as the object of the reference. His name is included in the logical connection between any later direct reference to him and Aristotle himself, that is, a connection according to Kripke's theory of such a historical-causal chain of references leading back to him. The identical object is both the object of a direct reference and the object in the causal origin of its being directly referred to. And reverting to our discussion of Quine's notion of objective empirical meaning, the independent object that is causally responsible for an utterance of an expression of a native speaker being subject to what Quine calls a "radical translation"—a translation between expressions of different languages without any common root or cognate—is a *certain* object— it is specified as the stimulation that, loosely said, is the "cause" of the utterance of its own expression that is prompted by the linguist's query.[8] Finally, an action, again as I am arguing Kant understands the concept according to his causal theory of the concept of the subtype in which the will is sufficient to play its logically required role in the causal origin of an action, is causally attributed to the will that is thereby logically determined, or bound, by the action.

This subtype of causal theory will be central to our concerns in what follows, since we are primarily concerned with Kant's causal theory of action in his moral thought, though the type that includes events will also come in for consideration when we discuss in more detail Kant's distinction between actions and events, as will actions that are not causal consequences of the will that conform to Kant's causal theory of action, since no *practical* causal law connects the will and its action in such cases. But, as stated in 1.1., Kant uses a notion of action that is much wider than that which constitutes his causal theory of action. Although his notion of an action in general contains the common feature that its independent object is the will, his varieties of action divide in certain ways that are orthogonal to each other.[9] First, Division I, there are actions that are *effects of the will*, and among these there are, first, Section A, actions that conform to Kant's causal theory of action, and, second, Section B, those that do not conform to the theory. Section A contains all and only actions produced by the will that are constituted by maxims that are enacted, or activated, by the will in its causal role in bringing about the actions, whereas those in Section B occur in *ordinary* or *physical causations*, in which the will brings about an action independently of any causal relation between the will and any maxim of the action. Another significant difference between Sections A and B of Division I is that in Section A, the will is not the effect of or conditioned by an external object or condition with respect to its causal efficacy regarding its action, whereas in Section B the causal efficacy of the will with respect to its action is itself the effect of or conditioned by an external object or condition. In addition to Division I, there is Division II, which includes all and only actions that are ascribed to the will through their respective maxims. Division II is also divided into two sections. Section A of Division II contains all and only actions that belong to Section A of Division I, whereas those that are *not* effects of the will constitute Section B. To sum up, all and only actions that conform to Kant's causal theory of action belong to both Divisions of action. They are what I consider Kant's "basic" actions and the only ones that are subject to moral judgment and therefore consti-

---

8 W. V. O. Quine, *Word and Object*, p. 30.
9 Applications of the typology of actions that follows will be given later, in 3.2. and 3.3.

tute the central interest of this book. Actions in Division I, Section B, which are only the effects of natural forces, including the agent's psychological make-up, cannot coherently be subjected to moral judgment, nor can actions in Division II, Section B, which can be ascribed to the will through the maxims of the agent, but do not causally depend on the will. It is the causality of the will with respect to its actions, and therefore its freedom, that alone belongs to both Divisions of action and is accordingly basic to Kant's conception of action according to which it is subject to moral judgment. That is why the central interest of my book consists in all and only actions that conform to Kant's causal theory of action, and why his idea of the freedom of the will is to be understood as the primary consequence of that theory.

Finally, our discussion thus far has been full enough, however, to merit calling independent objects that answer to the subtype of causal theory just introduced—the subtype according to which the independent objects are specified or given according to the concepts of their respective effects—actions, memories, writings of history, direct references and prompted utterances on occasions of translation—*internal objects*, since they stand in contrast to *external objects*, which can only be specified or given independently of their effects and therefore specified or given independently of the *logical* connection between themselves and the concept of their effects. For since their specifications cannot be specified or given as part of the specification of their effects, they can be empirically determined or identified only on the basis of experience or perception, as they must be in the case of the specification of a cause of a given effect that is an *event* in an ordinary or physical causation, as Kant understands the term.

These last points can be reconnected to the issue of single-object versus dual-object ontology discussed earlier. Single-object ontology is the operative ontology iff the independent object, i.e. the object playing a role in the causal origin of a given effect, is specified or given and is included in the logical connection between the cause and the effect; otherwise more than one object is involved, as is the case in the subtype of a causal theory of an event (since the causality of an event depends on the causality of another event that is unspecified or merely thought, and hence that can be specified or given only through experience or an independent perception). Therefore, iff specification of the cause is included in the logical connection between the cause and the effect, the cause and its effect are an identical object that has both aspects or is viewed both ways: cause and effect. The object of a perception and its cause are two aspects of an identical object, viz. the perceived object, which is specified or given. It is both perceived, or the object of the perception, and the cause of its being perceived, or the cause of its being the object of the perception. Thus it causes itself to be perceived, or causes itself to be the object of the perception, provided of course that the cause affects a perceiver, who definitely is not another object in the causation. An object of a memory and its causal antecedent are two aspects of an identical object, the remembered object—the cause of the object of the memory and the effect of the cause, i.e. the object of the memory. It is both remembered and the causal origin of its being so. Gibbon's writing his history of the decline and fall of Rome and its causal antecedent, i.e. the decline and fall of Rome, are two aspects of an identical object, viz., the historical event written about by Gibbon. It is both the object of Gibbon's writing and the causal origin of its being so. An object of direct reference and its causal antecedent are two aspects of an identical object—Aristotle directly referred to. The object directly referred to, i.e. Aristotle, is both the object of the direct reference and the causal origin of its being so. An affirmative or negative response and its prompt "Gavagai?" when coupled with a given stimulation are two aspects of a single object, the stimulation meant by the response and thus by the utterance of the expression. It is both the object of the response or the utterance of the expression and the causal origin of its being so. Finally, an action of the will and its causal origin are two aspects of the identical will: it is *both* logically determined or *bound* by the action *and* the cause of its being so.

1.5 Summary of the Scope and Limits of the Book

These, then, are the central as well as certain subsidiary concepts and concerns that are taken up in the work that follows. As I have already acknowledged, the limitation on the scope and extent of the work as dictated by its limited objective —an enhanced sympathetic understanding of Kant's metaethics, especially his concept of the freedom of the will as a necessary condition of the possibility of the objectivity of morality, that is, moral judgment—keeps the work from engaging in any extended discussion of his normative ethics. The intention is that this limited scope, rather than constitute a shortcoming of the essay, will instead, adapted as it is to the notion of causality belonging to Grice's causal theory of perception—a notion that is generally acknowledged by analytic philosophers as at least meeting the standards of philosophical intelligibility, if not universal acceptance—increases the chances of a more sympathetic understanding of Kant's notion of the freedom of the will among these same philosophers, including especially, of course, those who are Kant scholars.

2 Causal Theories of Objects and Grice's Causal Theory of Perception

2.1 Introduction

In addition to its being a causal interpretation of Kant's concept of an *action done by a subject*, or an *agent*, I have said that this book is also a causal interpretation of his concepts of *appearance* and *event*. I call this way of interpreting a concept "*a causal theory*" of the object so conceived, e.g., a causal theory of an action, an appearance, or an event, because the concept logically requires the existence of an independent object—the subject of an action, the object that appears in an appearance, or the preceding event that results in the event so conceived—play a role in the causal origin of the object so conceived.

Historically, causal theories of objects are not limited to Kant. Locke had a causal theory of ideas of physical objects—specifically, ideas of sensation—since their concept—the concept of a sensory idea of an object— logically requires the object to play a role in bringing about the idea—the sensation. In contemporary analytic philosophy, again as stated in the previous chapter, H. P. Grice has resuscitated "the causal theory of perception"[1]—perception of a material object—after a period of its languishing in philosophical disrepute, and P. F. Strawson has followed Grice in this endeavor, but with a modification to the theory.[2]

The idea that the concept of a perception of a material object logically requires the object to bring about the sense-data that constitute the object's own perception is the point of departure of my exposition of Kant's concepts of *appearance* and *event*, and above all, *action*. It is chosen to play this role, again as I said earlier, because it is formulated in terms of a contemporary causal theory that has proved to be valuable, and even celebrated, in discussion of perception among analytic philosophers despite its apparent problems. Given Kant's critics' charge that his causal theory of action creates suspicion of the philosophical value of his notion of pure, i.e. non-empirical, atemporal causality, and thus the *non-natural* causality of his idea of the freedom of the will, suspicion such as Wood's, cited in the Preface,

---

[1] H. P. Grice, "The Causal Theory of Perception," *Proceedings of the AristotelianSociety,Supplementary Volumes*, XXXV (1961).
[2] P. F. Strawson, "Causation in Perception," in *Freedom and Resentment and Other Essays* (Oxford/NewYork, Routledge, 2008, first published, Methuen & Co., 1974), pp. 76–7, and "Perception and Its Objects," in *Knowledge: Readings in Contemporary Epistemology,"* ed. Sven Bernecker and Fred Dretske, first published in *Perception and Identity: Essays Presented to A. J. Ayer*, ed. G. F. Macdonald, (Oxford University Press, 2006), pp. 460–61.

the advantage of adapting Kant's causal theory of action to Grice's causal theory of perception is that we might thereby improve the chances of our giving Kant's theory of freedom a more positive assessment. Grice's notion of the causality of the perceived object, moreover, seems to have escaped notice of what I think is its "non-natural" character, and therefore has escaped suspicion of its importance in that respect. If, then, an interpretation of Kant's causal theory of action can be adapted to Grice's causal theory of perception, and Grice's can remain philosophically worthy despite its being shown to be non-natural in character, the philosophical value of Kant's theory might be viewed as partaking of the philosophical value of Grice's theory. Ground will have thus been laid for an interpretation of Kant's causal theory of action that might mitigate, if not allay, suspicion about its value. As a consequence, one ground for a more positive valuation of Kant's theory of *morality* will also have been laid, since the freedom of the will is, again, as Kant himself says, the "keystone" of his "entire edifice" (KpV 5:4). Of course, there is the possibility that a demonstration of any non-natural character of Grice's theory will cast suspicion on that theory as well. Since Grice's theory has continued to receive esteem despite its apparent problems, perhaps it can be deemed valuable even in terms of empiricist constraints of analytic philosophy, thereby indicating that analytic philosophy may not be as empirically constrained as it has so far been thought to be.

The plan I will follow is, first, to discuss Grice's proposal of the necessary and sufficient conditions for his elucidation, or analysis, of what he considers to be our ordinary concept of a perception of a material object, or, to put it another way, the conditions of a *complete* theory of such a perception. He argues that it is *necessary* that the material object play a role in the causal origin of the perception. Since generally other objects besides the material object in question are also not just causally required by such a perception, but can fairly be said to be perceived as well, say, a lamp required for light on a book lying on a desk, then, since they are not the object in question, the causality of these other causally involved objects must be ruled out by the analysis of the concept. That is, Grice must *isolate* the causality of the perceived object from the causality of other objects that are also causally involved in the existence of a perception, but which are not the object in question, and this task of isolation belongs to a *constraint* on the objects causally involved.

Grice's constraint is that the perceived object is of the kind whose members are perceived by perceivers through such sensory states—called "sense-data" in a special sense explained by Grice—as those that are *the empirical constituents* that, in that sense, *empirically constitute* the perception of the object: they are the empirical or material elements of which the perception of the object empirically consists. This constraint, however, confronts the obvious objection of circularity, made by P. F. Strawson[3] and continued by A. J. Ayer.[4] The circularity prevents Grice's theory of perception from being complete, since the theory cannot provide the *sufficient* as well as the necessary conditions constituting an analysis of the concept. Strawson tries to correct for the circularity and thus provide the *sufficient* as well as the necessary conditions in question by doing two things. He first specifies the perceived object, which makes it *given*, and not merely thought,[5] thereby avoiding Grice's problem of trying to distinguish the object from other causes of the perception in terms of the causal efficacy objects of the *same kind* as the perceived object have with respect to such a perception—an attempt foiled by the circularity that the kind in question logically depends on the nature of the sense-data that a perceiver would get from objects of that kind. And, second, he accordingly shifts the discussion from the restriction on the kind of causality that is specific to the perceived *object* to his own restrictions on the "correct description" of the *experience* brought about by the object in the perceiver (where Strawson's "experience" performs the role of Grice's "sense-data") and that having been so brought about constitutes the object's perception. Where Grice's condition had to isolate the *object* from among all objects that would be *causally* required by the existence of a perception of the object, Strawson's analysis of the same concept first isolates the object through a specification that distinguishes the object from other objects that would also be causally involved in the existence of a perception of the object in question and might also be perceived, but would not be the perceived object in question,[6] and then Strawson puts constraints on the description of the *experience* that constitutes the perception of the object, which distinguish the description from other descriptions of experiences that a subject may "enjoy" (Strawson's expression) on an occasion of a perception of the object but are not the specific experience that constitutes the perception of the object.[7] Strawson thus needs conditions in his analysis of the concept of perception that must be met by the description of the *experience*, if the experience is to count as a perception of the perceived object, conditions that effectively exclude other objects that are also causally involved in the perception—objects whose causal involvement in the perception,

---

3 Strawson, "Causation in Perception," p. 80–1.
4 A. J. Ayer, "The Causal Theory of Perception," *Proceedings of the Aristotelian Society, Supplementary Volumes* LI (1977), pp. 113–14
5 The application to Strawson of the distinction between an object's being given and its being thought is introduced in 1.4.
6 This would be like Quine's "collateral information," such as Donald Davidson's rabbit-fly briefly discussed below in n.15.
7 Strawson, *"Perception and Its Objects,"* p. 461.

though *causally* necessary for the *existence* of the perception, are not *logically* required by the concept of a perception of an object nor are they even *causally* required by the experience that constitutes the perception—an essential property of Grice's and Strawson's causal theories of perception that distinguishes causations in perception from ordinary causations. Where an object in an *ordinary* causation can either enable or block a *perception*, it cannot enable or block the *sense-data* (Grice) or *experience* (Strawson) that constitutes the perception of the object. Indeed, neither the sense-data nor the experience that constitute a perception of their causes can play *any* role as an *effect* in an *ordinary* causation, although they *must* play such a role in a causation in perception. Equivalently, an ordinary cause cannot play a role in the causal origin of sense-data or an experience that constitute a perception of the cause; only a cause in a causation in perception can do that.

It is the requirement of this further condition for a complete analysis of our causal concept of a perception of a material object, or for a complete causal theory of such a perception, a desideratum of both Grice's and Strawson's theories, that will guide the further course of this book. The point to keep in mind throughout is the need for a specification of any such further condition so that a complete causal theory of the *effect* of a cause can be achieved. It will be the idea that leads to Kant's theory of the *maxim* of an action as a necessary condition which, when combined with his theory of the freedom of the will as the other necessary condition of an action, when the will alone can be causally connected to the action through the Categorical Imperative, provides the necessary and sufficient conditions for the causality of the will to be necessary for the existence of an action, and thus completes the interpretation of Kant's causal theory of action.

2.2 Grice's Basic Idea

Grice's basic idea is that our concept of a perception of a material object logically requires, not just that the object exists, which many philosophers might readily concede, but that it play a role in the causal origin of the perception. Since a causal relation obtains only between logically distinct existences, Grice posits sense-data as the *effect* that is distinct from the object that plays this role in the causal origin of a perception. But Grice's sense-data are not the classical sense-data of the 17th and 18th Centuries, with their colors, shapes, sounds, tactile feelings, and other sensations as well. They are rather its sensibly seeming to the perceiver if she were perceiving the object, and this would entail how it looks—its appearance—to her. All this would be expressed by an ordinary description of the object, with the essential caveat that the description describes merely its sensibly seeming to the perceiver as if she were perceiving the object. It would be a description of the perceptual state she would be in under that condition—a description of the effect of the object on her senses. For example, it would be a description of its sensibly seeming to her *as if* she were seeing a book on the desk. Grice uses the old nomenclature of *sense-data* to designate this appearance as he understands it, and the existence of the sense-data is the effect—the effect on the perceiver—that is logically distinct from the existence of its cause. Now, the crucial part of Grice's causal theory of perception—his basic idea—is that something is a perception of an object only if the object plays a role in the causal origin of the sense-data that constitute the perception—the data that are the empirical constituents, or material content, of the perception. The novelty of his formulation of the causal theory of perception is that the *logical*, i.e. non-causal, relation of the concept of a perception of a material object to the existence of the object includes the *causal*, i.e. *non-logical*, relation between the existence of the object and that of the sense-data that constitute the perception. The *causal*, i.e. non-logical, relation therefore constitutes the *causal* dependence of a perception on the object, a *causal dependence* that is *logically required* by the concept of a perception of such an object, in the sense that the concept contains the causal dependence, and where the perception consists of the very sense-data that causally depend on the object, and therefore sense-data whose own concept, *unlike* the concept of the *perception*, is *logically distinct* from the object.

According to Grice's analysis, therefore, the concept of sense-data is logically *distinct* from the object on which the sense-data *causally depend*, and the concept of the perception contains that causal dependence. This is not to suggest a philosophical difficulty. It is only to draw attention to a consequence of Grice's theory, viz., that the concept of the *causal connection* between the existence of an object and that of certain sense-data entails that the effect, i.e. the sense-data, *is* distinct from that of its cause and that the *logical* connection between the concept of the *perception* of a material object and the existence of the object entails that the concept *is not* distinct from the object that is a cause of the existence of the object conceived, i.e. the perception. In this manner, the causal, i.e. non-logical, connection between the sense-data and their cause is *included* in the logical, i.e. non-causal, connection between the *concept* of a perception of such a material object and the object, which therefore can play a role in the causal origin of the perception of the object.

Grice and Strawson's inclusion of a causal connection in a logical connection can be seen as a certain distinction between first- and second-orders of proposition and the corresponding nature of the causality involved in their respective causal theories of perception. In an ordinary causation, an antecedent causal connection would itself be a causal condition of a subsequent further effect. Fire would produce smoke that would produce damaged goods. But in a causation in perception, the causal dependence of certain sense-data or a certain experience on the perceived object is not itself a causally necessary condition of the effect, i.e. the perception. It is rather a logically necessary condition for the sense-data or the experience *to be* a perception of the object. The causal dependence of the data or the experience on the perceived object is a higher- or second-order rule or condition contained in the concept of a perception of an object—a rule or a condition that determines the data or the experience belong to or instantiate a perception of the object—a lower-or first-order proposition. The second-order proposition does not causally connect the object to the perception. The causal dependence of the data or the experience on the object is rather a second-order rule or condition for the data or the experience to be a proper *subject* of a first-order ascription of the concept of a perception. It would be a causal consequence of the perceived object only in the sense that the sense-data or the experience that *constitute* the perception—its sensory material or content—causally depend on the perceived object, but the perception does not causally depend on the object in the sense that the perception causally depends on its sensory material or content, which do causally depend on the object, since the perception definitely does *not* causally depend on its constituent data or experience. To sum up, Grice and Strawson's are causal theories of perception can be seen as second-order causal theories of first-order *ascriptions* of the concept of a perception to given sense-data or an experience.[8]

2.3 A Consequence of Grice's Theory

As stated, Grice's theory holds that the concept of a perception of a material object logically requires that the object play a role in the causal origin of the sense-data that constitute its perception, or more simply, it is logically required that the object play a role in the causal origin of its perception. But since necessarily, the object would be perceived if it were to cause its perception (and hence, if its perception were to exist), the object would be logically required to play a role in the causal origin of *its* being perceived, i.e. the *object's* being perceived; that is, it would be required to play a role in the causal origin of a perception of itself. Although the causal theory requires that the perceived object play this role, it must be admitted that the perceived object cannot be perceived in its enactment of this role. Otherwise, its

---

8 This point about second- and first-orders of proposition resumes the discussion of the same point in the Preface as it there concerned Kant's causal theory of action.

being perceived would causally depend on its being perceived, which, being circular, would make it impossible for the causal connection between the object and its perception to be a *condition* for the sense-data to be a perception of the object. Hence, it is only seemingly paradoxical to conclude that the perceived object must exist apart from being perceived, that is, that it exist unperceived, for its imperceptibility would simply and non-paradoxically be a logical consequence of the object's playing the role Grice's causal theory assigns to it. If we consider the object in the respect that it is the object that has this causal efficacy regarding sense-data that constitute its perception, it can be called the *agent* that brings about the perception of the object whose concept contains the agent. The agent, being a cause from which its effect must be distinct, would be *imperceptible*. Although the perceived object would obviously remain perceived, and therefore perceptible, its concept would logically entail that its agency—a causal property of the perceived object—would be imperceptible. Thus, there is the consequence of Grice's causal theory of perception—the consequence that is referred to by the title of this section of the chapter—that *the cause of an effect cannot be perceived independently of the effect*. Apart from its effect, it is imperceptible. It is precisely this consequence that Grice was apparently trying to circumvent when he committed the circularity that Strawson and Ayer correctly fault him for in his attempt to isolate the perceived object from among other objects that also play a role in the causal origin of a perception.

My analysis of *Grice's causal theory* of perception itself gives the same result as Grice's own analysis of *the concept* of a perception of a material object. Since according to Grice's theory a perception of material object is the effect of the object, it is impossible for the object to be perceived independently of its effect, or its effects (if more than one effect is said to possibly result from the action of the object). That is, it is analytic that the object cannot be perceived independently of its effect(s). Since the object that is determined through its causal property, viz., the property that is determinative of the agent, is causally independent of its effect(s), and the theory of perception is causal, the agent cannot be perceived independently of its effect. That is precisely the same result that was derived from the argument that immediately preceded it, only now it has been derived from an analysis of Grice's causal theory of perception, i.e. a second-order analysis of his analysis of his concept of such a perception, instead of directly from the analysis itself. The identity of the results from the two analyses should not be surprising since, if the analysis of Grice's theory is accurate, it would comprehend exactly what his theory analyzes as the content or the entailment(s) of the concept of perception.

Despite the nomenclature, however, we will still encounter awkward uses of the terms "perceived object," where the perceived object will need to be the agent of the perceived object's being perceived but also where it cannot be the agent, since it is perceived. It is hoped that the contexts in which the uses occur will be helpful in removing confusions.

2.4 A Contrast Between Causation in Perception and Ordinary Causation Based on This Consequence of Grice's Theory, i.e. the Imperceptibility of the Agent

This imperceptibility of the agent contrasts with the perceptibility of an object whose effect is *not* a perception of the object, but is rather an ordinary effect, that is, an effect in what Grice considers an "ordinary" causation, where "perception of the object" is understood according to Grice's causal theory of perception. To cite Grice's own example of an ordinary causation, consider the causal connection between some smoke and a fire based on the causal inference of fire from smoke, itself based on the correlation of frequent occurrences of smoke and fire.[9] The cause of the smoke can be perceived independently of the smoke. This way of drawing the contrast between causation in perception and ordinary causation has a significant consequence of its own. Whereas there can be no perception of the perceived object in its role in the causal origin of the perception, and therefore no perception of the perceived object that is independent of its effect on Grice's causal theory of perception, a cause of an effect in an *ordinary* causation *can* be perceived independently of the effect. So, in neither case—neither in causation in perception nor in ordinary causation—can an effect be a perception of a cause through any sense-data that constitute the perception: the smoke cannot be a perception of the fire nor can a perception of the fire be a perception of any role of the fire in the causal origin of the perception that is constituted by the sense-data that causally depend on the object. To sum up, the perception of a cause in an ordinary causation cannot be understood in the same way that a perception of an object in a causation in perception can be understood according to Grice's causal theory of perception. Since our interest is in Grice's causal theory of perception, let us bypass the question of whether a causal theory of perception *other than* Grice's could account for a perception of a cause in an ordinary causation and simply presume that a perception of an ordinary cause can be understood only according to a *non-causal* theory of perception: a theory of perception of an object that is the cause of an effect in an ordinary causation, where, therefore, the effect is not a perception of the object,

---

9 Grice, "The Causal Theory of Perception," p. 149.

where "perception" is understood according to Grice's causal theory of perception.

There are of course many such theories available, but it seems that a thread that runs through enough of them to be considered a common theme is that a condition for sense-data to be a perception of an object is that the *subject*, i.e. the *percipient*, *thinks* the sense-data through our ordinary concepts of objects. In the history of early modern philosophy, the relation that thinking objects through such concepts bears to the sense-data that are thought customarily goes by the name of *imagination*. From there it is a short step to our using the concepts to make *judgments* about objects in the world. Thus, in a historically classical *non-causal* theory of perception it is the action, or imagination, of the thinking *subject* that orders the sense-data as a perception of an object according to our ordinary concepts of objects, whereas in Grice's causal theory of perception it is the action of the *object* that makes the data qualified as a perception of the object. In a *non-causal* theory of perception the data are, well, *given* (as described in 1.4, viz. specified independently of being thought), and a logically necessary condition for the data to be a perception of an object is the *subject's thinking* the data through its ordinary concepts of objects, whereas in Grice's causal theory of perception it is the *object's* playing a role in the causal origin of the data that is a logically necessary condition for the data to be a perception of the object. Thus does one theory of perception get the name "causal" and the other theory "non-causal."[10]

Imagination cannot be a condition for sense-data to be a perception of an ordinary object in a non-causal theory of perception, however, unless the data and the thinking subject, like the agent and the sense-data the agent produces in Grice's causal theory of perception, are logically distinct from each other. Imagination is a non-logical, and in that sense "causal," relation between the given and thought (although the theory still qualifies as "non-causal" because of its contrast with the already denominated "causal theory of perception"). Yet this is precisely the classical distinction of sense-data from thought through our ordinary concepts of objects that Grice eschews in his *causal* theory of perception, and with his eschewal, the necessary disavowal of imagination as the logically required connection that makes sense-data a perception of an ordinary object in a *non-causal* theory of perception. As we saw at the start of our discussion, Grice employs our ordinary concepts of objects to describe *sense-data* and invokes the language of seeming, appearance, or looks in order to capture the distinctness of sense-data from our *judgments* about the world, but not the clas-

---

10 A case in point is Kant's non-causal theory of perception introduced at B 160.

sical distinctness of sense-data from our *thought* about the world. But since he has a *causal* theory of perception that involves sense-data that are *already* characterized by our ordinary concepts of object, and thus a *causal* theory that already employs thought through such concepts, it seems that such thought cannot independently play its classical role as a logically necessary *condition* for sense-data to be perceptions of objects of ordinary causations in any *non-causal* theory of perception he might consider adopting. In a word, Grice's causal theory of perception co-opts thought through our ordinary concepts of objects and thus keeps it (or imagination) from playing its customary role in any non-causal theory of perception that he might adopt. Sense-data ordered *from the beginning* by thought for the sake of a *causal* theory of perception cannot then somehow be scrambled and available *de novo* in a "primitive" state that would *precede* the aforementioned *beginning* of Grice's causal theory of perception, all for the sake of a *non-causal* theory of perception.[11]

To review, the non-causal theories under consideration are all based on distinguishing within a perception what is empirically *given* from what is *thought* through our ordinary concepts of objects, where the given is considered to be in some sense more "primitive" than what is involved in our ordinary concepts —the concepts that we use to make judgments about the world, and hence concepts that belong to our relatively more sophisticated "theory" of the world. So, what is empirically given in a perception is distinct from what is thought, leaving to thought the necessary supplement of the given that allows for the combination of the two in the perception of an object of an ordinary concept, and thus allows for a judgment about the world based on the perception of the object.

This consequence of Grice's theory can be summarized, and Grice's distinction between causation in perception and ordinary causation can be reiterated in terms of the summary. If the concept of an effect allows the object that causes the effect to be perceived independently of the effect, the effect *cannot* be a perception of the object through the sense-data that constitute a perception according to the causal efficacy of the object with respect to them; so, by transposition, if an effect *can* be a perception of the object that causes it with respect to its constituent sense-data, the object cannot be perceived independently of its effect.

---

11 Strawson's version of the causal theory of perception faces the same problem as Grice's. See Strawson's "Imagination and Perception," in *Freedom and Resentment*, pp. 50–72, first published in *Experience and Theory*, ed. Lawrence Foster and J. W. Swanson, (Amherst, MA: University of Massachusetts Press, 1970). Strawson may not have seen this problem when he came to publish his adoption of the basic idea of Grice's causal theory of perception ("Causation in Perception"), especially including the role of our ordinary concepts of objects in our "correct descriptions" of our experiences that are perceptions of the objects.

Accordingly, a causation in perception would be a causation in which the concept of the effect *prohibits* an independent perception of the object that causes the effect in the respect specified, which would be the *agent* that was introduced above, whereas an ordinary causation would be one in which the concept of the effect *allows* a perception of the object that causes the effect, where the perception would be independent of the effect of the object. It is this difference between *prohibition* and *allowance* of a perception of the object that causes the effect in the respect specified, and thus where the perception is independent from the effect of the object, that can summarize a ground for Grice's distinction between the two causations (one concept of perception per type of causation).

2.5 A Second Consequence of Grice's Theory[12]

A second consequence of Grice's causal theory of perception is that a perceived object cannot be an effect of or conditioned by another object—an external object—with respect to the perceived object's causal efficacy regarding the sense-data that constitute its perception. The consequence can be stated positively, viz., the perceived object is causally efficacious regarding the sense-data that constitute its perception only if its causal efficacy in that respect is self-sufficient.

An indirect argument for this second consequence of Grice's causal theory of perception can be given. If a perceived object were to causally depend on another object with respect to the perceived object's causal connection to the sense-data that constitute its perception, it would count *against* bringing the perception of the object under Grice's causal theory of perception and instead would count for bringing it under a *non-causal* theory of perception. For, in the context of Grice's causal theory, if the sense-data that constitute the perception of the perceived object were to causally depend on another object, the data, and thus the perception of the perceived object, would be affected by the other object, and therefore would not be the data, and thus would not be the perception, that they (and the perception) would have been if the data (and hence the perception) had been unaffected by the other object and the perceived object had instead been self-sufficient in its bringing about the sense-data that constitute its perception. In other words, if another object besides the perceived object were causally involved in the existence of the sense-data that constitute the perception of the perceived object, there would be a *discrepancy* or a *mismatch* between the data and the perceived object, since the

---

[12] Thanks to Jeremy Fantl for some long discussions and very helpful comments on this section of the chapter, 2.5.

other object's causal involvement would be reflected in the data. In that sense, the perception of the perceived object could be said to be *distorted by* or *mixed with* the other object's effect on the causal efficacy of the perceived object with respect to the perceived object's effect, viz., the sense-data that would constitute its perception. Again, its sensibly seeming to the perceiver as if she were perceiving the object, and therefore the perception of the object, would not be what it would have been if the perceived object had been self-sufficient, in the sense of its being causally independent of another object in its causal connection with the sense-data that constitute its perception.

A non-modal indirect argument can also be given. If an object besides the perceived object were to affect the sense-data that constitute the perception of the perceived object, and thus affect its perception, it would confound the implication that the perception would identify the perceived object, since the data that would constitute the perception would causally depend on the *other* object. If, on the other hand, the other object's effect on the perceived object were to make no sensory, and hence no perceptual, difference, to the perceived object's causal efficacy with respect to the data that constitute the perceived object's perception, the question of the perceived object's causal dependence on another object regarding the former's causal connection with the sense-data that constitute its perception would be moot.

On the other hand, if the other object were not to be comprised by the perceived object, and the perceived object *were* to causally depend on the other object for its causal efficacy regarding its own effect, and confounding the reference of the perception to just the perceived object were to be *avoided*, a theory of the perception would have to be switched from Grice's causal theory to a *non-causal* theory of perception. On the latter theory, not only does the perceived object's causal dependence on another object not confound the perception of the perceived object, since the sense-data that constitute a perception of the object do not causally depend on *any* object—the perceived object or any other object—the theory actually *requires* the perceived object's causal dependence on another object, if it is to be a theory of a perception of an object in an ordinary causation. Obviously, on a non-causal theory of perception, an *effect* of a perceived object could not be the *sense-data* that constitute the perception of the perceived object; otherwise, the perception would conform to Grice's causal theory of perception. These points can be illustrated by examples of other causal theories of objects, most of which come from the previous chapter, which cited Strawson as their source,[13] but Strawson does not make quite the same use of them as is done here.

2.6 Applications of the Second Consequence of Grice's Theory[14]

Addressing perception first, let an airplane that is overhead of a perceiver play a role in the causal origin of her perception of the plane by playing a role in the causal origin of *its sensibly seeming to her as if she were seeing the plane*. Then, if its sensibly seeming to her as if she were seeing the plane were to causally depend on its being *overhead*, her perception of the *plane* would be confounded by its *being overhead*; otherwise, its being overhead would not affect its sensibly seeming to her as if she were seeing the *plane*. On the other hand, if its sensibly seeming to her as if she were seeing the plane *were* to causally depend on its being overhead and the perception's being confounded were to be avoided, the theory of the perception would have to be changed from Grice's causal theory to a *non-causal* theory of perception. On the latter theory, the plane's causal efficacy regarding its own effect could causally depend on some object or condition, such as its being overhead, without creating a problem for the theory like the confounding of the perception, since the sense-data that constitute a perception of the plane would not causally depend on *any* object or condition of the object—the plane or any external condition of its causal efficacy with respect to its seeming to the perceiver as if she were seeing the plane, such as its being overhead.

A second illustration of the point would be a Gricean-type causal theory of memory.[15] Let its sensibly seeming to someone as if she were remembering a certain concert causally depend on when the concert occurred. This would confound her memory of the concert, since the memory of the concert would not then be a memory of just the concert, but of something else as well, viz., when it occurred. It would be the influence of when the concert occurred on its sensibly seeming to the concert-goer as if she were remembering the concert that would confound the memory of the concert. However, the memory might in-

---

13 Strawson, "Causation in Perception" and "Perception and Its Objects."
14 Reading these applications might be facilitated by keeping in mind the variety of actions—their Divisions, I and II, and Sections, A and B—that was introduced in Section 4 of the previous chapter.
15 Use of the following considerations pertaining here to just memory will be applied to memory of action that conforms to Kant's causal theory of action in 4.2 below, where just his causal theory of action apart from any memory of an action will be presented in 3.2. below.

2.6 Applications of the Second Consequence of Grice's Theory — 27

stead consist of its sensibly seeming to her as if she were remembering *when the concert occurred*, in which case it *would* be a memory of *when the concert occurred*. If so, the memory *would* conform to a causal theory of memory and would not be confounded by when it occurred.

On the other hand, when the concert occurred would present no such problem for a *non-causal* theory of a memory of the concert, and the confounding of the memory would be avoided. For then when it occurred could affect the concert's bringing about a memory, in case it in fact brought about a memory, which, moreover, might or might not be a memory of the concert. But in that case neither the concert nor when it occurred would be *causally* connected to *its sensibly seeming to the concert-goer as if she were remembering (a) the concert* or *(b) when it occurred*, if its sensibly seeming to the concert-goer as if she were remembering either (a) or (b) constituted a memory of either (a) or (b), since, *ex hypothesi*, *its sensibly seeming ...etc.* would be given to the concert-goer according to a *non-causal* theory of memory, and on such a theory *its sensibly seeming ...etc.* could *not* be causally attributed to the remembered object or when it occurred in the first place. In such a case of conformity to a *non-causal* theory of memory, there might actually be *two* memories: the first memory would be the *causal consequence* of the concert, and the concert would itself have been a causal consequence of when the concert occurred. No philosophical *theory* of memory involving *its seeming to the concert-goer as if she were perceiving the concert* would account for *this* memory of the concert, since the memory would be an effect in an *ordinary causation*, the efficient cause of which would be the concert, and the effect would be the memory of the concert, without its being a memory of the concert through its seeming to the concert-goer as if she were remembering the concert. Without a theory of the memory in terms of such mental states of the concert-goer, the concert could indeed help or interfere with the existence of the memory, but neither the concert nor any object or condition affecting it could have any effect on the existence of *its seeming to the concert-goer as if she were remembering the concert*. The causal efficacy of the concert with respect to the effect that is a memory in such an *ordinary causation* of a memory stops at the threshold of merely enabling or disabling the mere existence of the *memory* of the concert in the concert-goer, but it cannot cross the threshold and affect the content of the memory, viz., *its seeming to the concert-goer as if she were remembering the concert*, in the sense in which the concert does affect *its seeming to the concert-goer as if she were remembering the concert* on a *causal theory of memory*. To repeat, the concert's causal efficacy stops at the existence of the memory without affecting its content. That is why, if the *effect* of the concert is a memory of the concert in an ordinary causation, and thus would be independent of this causal theory of memory, there could be no implication that it is a memory of specifically the concert or a memory of anything that could be specified merely on the basis of the fact that the concert enabled or interfered with the concert-goer's having the memory, i.e. the existence of the memory. These restrictions would be part of what it means for the concert and its effect, i.e. the memory of the concert, to belong to an *ordinary* causation, and thus distinct from the causation involved in this causal theory of memory.

The *other* memory mentioned above would be the memory of the concert that brings about its effect, which might be the first mentioned memory of the concert, and it *would* indeed be causally related back to when the concert occurred. This other memory of the concert *could* then be accounted for on a *non-causal* theory of memory. In that case, *its sensibly seeming to the concert-goer as if she were remembering the concert* would constitute the memory of the concert, but the memory would not causally depend on the concert, nor would it causally depend on when it occurred, nor, again, would it causally depend on any object or external condition. Hence, this memory of the concert would conform to a non-causal theory of memory, and would be a memory of the concert insofar as the concert causally stands between its own effect—which might be the other memory—the first mentioned memory—and its causal antecedent, e.g., when the concert occurred. In this second case of a memory, which conforms to a non-causal theory of memory, the remembered concert does causally depend on when it occurred, but when it occurred cannot confound the memory, since neither the concert nor when it occurred can affect the *content* of the memory, which would be *its sensibly seeming to the concert-goer as if she were remembering the concert*. In sum, *neither* the memory of the concert that conforms to a non-causal theory of memory *nor* the effect of the concert that is a memory in an *ordinary causation* (the first mentioned memory of the concert) can be confounded by when the concert occurred. In these last respects, both the memory of the concert on a non-causal theory of memory and the memory first mentioned, which was an effect in an ordinary causation, would be quite different from the memory of the concert on a *causal* theory of memory, since on a causal theory, the effect on the concert of when it occurred and thus the effect of when it occurred on the content of the memory of the concert would present a problem for the causal theory of memory, since it would confound the memory of the concert on the causal theory, and so the theory would somehow have to exclude the condition of when the concert occurred.

The third illustration of the point under discussion is a Gricean-type causal theory of Edward Gibbon's writing his history of the decline and fall of Rome. If that event causally depended on, say, certain divisions in Roman society, its seeming to Gibbon as if he were writing the history of that event would also causally depend on those divisions, and thus his writing would causally depend on those divisions. But that would confound his writing about the decline and fall of Rome, since the decline and fall of Rome is distinct from the divisions in Roman society and, moreover, his history must be able to include the divisions in explanation of the decline and fall, and not presume them from the start by embedding them in the object of his work, thereby begging the question of what his history, as distinct from its object, is supposed to provide the reader. The causal dependence, obviously on something other than the event written about, would confound the writing about the event, and thus be troublesome for a causal theory of the writing of the history.

On the other hand, the decline and fall of Rome's causal dependence on divisions in Roman society could be written about on a *non-causal* theory of historical writing without confounding the writing about the event and thus without being troublesome for the theory without confounding the writing about the event. On such a non-causal theory of historical writing, the decline and fall of Rome can be both an effect of or conditioned by divisions in Roman society and a cause of, say, the evacuation of Britain by Roman forces. Gibbon's writing his history of the event would thus be causally independent of the event. On such a non-causal theory of historical writing, the decline and fall of Rome, divisions in Roman society, and the evacuation of Roman forces from Britain would belong to a series of ordinary causations, extending both backward and forward in time from around but not after the time of the decline and fall of Rome, with no particular event that starts the series, such as would be required by Gibbon's writing his history on a *causal* theory of historical writing, a series that does start with the decline and fall of Rome.

The fourth illustration of the point being made would be a speaker's making a direct reference to Aristotle, say, by using his name, on Kripke's historical-causal chain theory of how that can happen after Aristotle's parents have dubbed him "Aristotle": his parents dub him "Aristotle" and a historical-causal chain of uses of his name causally connects any later use that occurs in the chain to the individual. Since the chain, and thus any direct reference to Aristotle in the chain, causally depends on him, and he causally depended on his parents' procreativity, the chain (and thus any direct references to him) would causally depend on his parents' procreativity. But that would confound the direct reference to him, since his parents' procreativity did not start the direct *references* to him—their dubbing did, and he was not an effect of or conditioned by their dubbing, as that would be meant by the consequence of Grice's theory that is under discussion, but he certainly played a role in the causal origin of the dubbing and the subsequent references to him—all that would create a problem for Kripke's historical-causal theory of a direct reference to Aristotle.

If one were to object that Kripke's theory does hold that a later direct reference to Aristotle does historically-causally originate with the parents' dubbing him "Aristotle," then, in reply it could be said that a causal condition on which the *dubbing* depends, such as *when* it occurred, would, like the time of the occurrence of the concert that proved troublesome for a causal theory of memory, since it confounded the memory of the concert, would similarly prove troublesome for Kripke's theory, since it would confound any direct reference to Aristotle that occurs in the chain. A direct reference to Aristotle on Kripke's historical-causal theory of a chain of such references to him starting with his parents' dubbing him "Aristotle" cannot causally depend on when the dubbing took place, if trouble is not to be created for Kripke's theory by confounding of a direct reference to Aristotle. For then, *when the dubbing took place* would have an effect on the links in the chain that starts with the dubbing and would confound the direct references to him, since any direct reference to him via the historical-causal chain beginning with his parents' dubbing him "Aristotle" or even a direct reference to the dubbing itself would be confounded by when the dubbing took place. Since it had to take place at some time or other, when it took place could not affect the links in the chain without confounding them. Again, if when it took place does not affect the references in the chain, the case is moot.

On the other hand, Aristotle can causally stand between his parents' procreativity or their dubbing him "Aristotle," on the one hand, and his effects, on the other, even in case one such effect is a reference to him; but if it were, it would not occur in a chain of direct references to him that conform to Kripke's historical-causal theory of direct reference. A reference to him standing between his effects and his causal antecedents would be a reference that conforms to a *non-causal* theory of reference—a so-called "description" theory of reference, following such theorists as Frege and Strawson, as the theory has been dubbed by direct reference theorists—and the causal series that includes him, his effects, and his causal antecedents would be a series of ordinary causations, not causations in a historical-causal chain of direct references. On such a non-causal theory of reference, Aristotle could be referred to as the author of the Nichomachean Ethics without confounding the reference and therefore without creating any problem for the theory.

A penultimate illustration of the point under discussion—the last being Kant's causal theory of action, which will be given in the next chapter—is Quine's causal theory of empirical meaning. The meaning of an expression in a language radically different from the linguist's language would be the same, if there is such a thing as synonymy, Quine avers, as a corresponding expression in the linguist's language, viz., the stimulation jointly received by a native speaker and a linguist on an occasion of radical translation, would be confounded if the stimulation causally depended on another object.[16] In such a circumstance, the native speaker might be disposed to respond to the linguist's query on the basis of "collateral information" involving the *other* object instead of on the basis of just the stimulation. In that circumstance, Quine "concedes" that the native speaker's linguistic disposition would be "impure,"[17] quite like my use of "confound" in regard to what the *other* object does to the perception and memory of, historical writing about, and direct reference to the *original* object in the previous four examples that illustrate my point. To repeat, the problem is created for causal theories of objects in general by the causal dependence of original objects on other objects.

On the other hand, a stimulation can causally stand between an effect—a native speaker's response to the linguist's query about the meaning of an expression—and an object on which the response causally depends—an object about which the native speaker has "collateral information." In this circumstance, the meaning of an expression that stands for the stimulation, that is, a *reference* to the stimulation, could be understood on a theory of meaning, or now, preferably, a theory of *reference*, without creating a problem for the theory and without confounding the meaning/reference, but only if it is a *non-causal* theory of meaning/reference. For this purpose, Quine proposes a "background language" in which a speaker can make a selection among mutually incompatible ways of referring to objects, including such an object as the stimulation under discussion. Thus Quine arrives at his famous "ontological relativity" of concepts of reference—a relativity to a selection in terms of such a background language.

2.7 The Logical Connection Between the Two Consequences of Grice's Theory As Applied to All the Examples

On the First Consequence of Grice's theory, admittedly liberally based on the theory when it is not about perception, but instead is about memory, *et al.*, objects that are perceived, remembered, written about, directly referred to, or meant cannot be perceived, *et al.* independently of the effects of the objects, since any perceptions, *et al.* would themselves *be* effects of the objects. On the other con-

---

16 W. V. O. Quine, *Word and Object*, (New York and London: MIT Press and John Wiley & Sons, 1960), pp. 37–8. Quine cites Donald Davidson's example of a rabbit-fly that always accompanies a rabbit and may very well be relied on by the native speaker when responding to the linguist's prompt of "Gavagai?" but is, nonetheless, not part of the meaning of the expression, i.e. the stimulation, and the linguist should not include it in his translation of the expression.
17 W. V. O. Quine, *Word and Object*, p. 39.

sequence of Grice's theory, also liberally based on the theory, perceived objects, *et al.* cannot be effects of or conditioned by *other* objects without confounding the perceptions, *et al.* of the original objects (see especially Quine's "collateral information"). The logical connection between the two consequences of Grice's theory is that the First Consequence, viz., that the perceived object cannot be perceived independently of its effect, entails that the perception of the object would be confounded by *another* object's affect on the perceived object's causal efficacy with respect to the sense-data that would constitute the perception of the perceived object, since the perceived object would be perceived through sense-data that causally depend on the *other* object. Hence, to avoid the confounding, the theory must exclude the possibility that another object can affect the causal efficacy of the perceived object with respect to the sense-data that constitute its perception. The Second Consequence of Grice's theory is precisely this exclusion of the causal efficacy of another object on the perceived object with respect to the latter's causal efficacy regarding the sense-data that constitute its perception. A non-causal theory of perception avoids the confounding, because a perception that conforms to a non-causal theory of perception would not causally depend on its object in the first place, and hence would not be affected by another object's effect on the perceived object's causal efficacy with respect to its *effect*, again, an effect that could *not* be the perceived object's own perception on *any theory of perception*, since *ex hypothesi* the theory of its perception would be non-causal.

The more logically technical connection between the two consequences of Grice's theory would be a certain conditional relation between them. If a perceived object, *et al. can* be an effect of or conditioned by another object *without* confounding its perception, *et al.* (denial of the Second Consequence), it *can* be perceived, *et al.* independently of its effect (denial of the First Consequence). This conditional statement, however, is just the specification of a *non-causal theory of perception*. The denial of this conditional statement would be the conditional statement, "if an object could *not* be perceived, *et al.* independently of its effect (i.e. the First Consequence), it could be an effect of or conditioned by another object, if that would confound the object's perception (the Second Consequence)". Therefore, we get the obvious result that the two theories of perception, *et al.* and their corresponding types of causation—causation in perception and ordinary causation—are contrary to each other.

2.8 Explanation of the Connection between the Two Consequences

The previous section gives a logical connection between the two consequences that have been derived from Grice's causal theory of perception. An explanation of the connection can be given in an even more general way than is done in the previous section. This would involve a theory involving just the relation of cause and effect, and thus may be more theoretically satisfying with respect to the level of the generality of an explanation than what has been given so far.

If we examine the Second Consequence we have drawn from Grice's theory, viz., that the perceived object cannot be an effect of or conditioned by another object with respect to the perceived object's causal efficacy regarding the sense-data that constitute its perception, we notice that the effect of the other object is an effect *on* the perceived object, specifically, on its causal efficacy regarding the sense-data that constitute its perception. The effect of the other object *on* the perceived object, however, would be a condition *of* the perceived object—a condition that has an effect on the perceived object's causal efficacy regarding the sense-data that constitute its perception—*an efficacy, therefore, that the perceived object therefore would not have on its own*; otherwise, the other object would not have had that particular effect on the perceived object. This condition of the perceived object that originates with the other object would be, in that sense of "originating with an object," an *external* causal antecedent of the sense-data's constituting a perception of the perceived object—external to the perceived object—and thus would need to be contrasted with the condition that belongs to the perceived object *on its own*, that is, that would belong to it causally independently of every other object, or that could be said to belong to it *internally*.

A causal condition in general, however, cannot be a causal antecedent of an effect unless it is distinct from the effect. Conversely, since the effect cannot *be* the condition, it must be distinct from the condition in respect of what excludes it from being the condition. Since the sense-data that constitute a perception of the object also causally depend on the (antecedent) condition of receptivity that belongs to the *perceiver*—henceforth called the *subjective condition*—as well as on the (antecedent) condition of the perceived *object*, whether the condition originates internally or externally—henceforth called the *objective condition*—the subjective condition of the perceiver cannot be the objective condition of the object. Since the perceived object plays a role in the causal origin of its perception, it must be distinct from the subjective condition of the perceiver, and thus distinct from the subjective condition of the perception. Consequently, no external object can have an effect on, and thereby objectively condition, a perceived object with respect to the latter's causal efficacy regarding the sense-data that causally depend on a subjective condition of the perceiver unless the objective condition is distinct from the subjective one. In other words, the perceived object must be *free*, or logically and causally independent, of the subjective condition on which the sense-data that constitute its perception causally depend. Reference to the perceived object must therefore be sufficiently general to be independent of the features of the sense-data that causally depend on the subjective condition of the perceiver and that constitute its perception.

The question arises, however, whether reference to the perceived object and its causal efficacy with respect to the sense-data that constitute its perception can be sufficiently general to be distinct from the subjective condition of the perceiver without also being distinct from the *external* objective condition of the perceived object, that is, the objective condition that causally depends on another object. If not, then the generality of the reference to the causal efficacy of the perceived object with respect to the sense-data that constitute its perception would distinguish the causal efficacy from both the subjective condition of the perceiver and the *external* objective condition of the perceived object. In other words, the generality of the causal efficacy of the perceived object would not distinguish between the *subjective* condition of the perceiver and the *external* objective condition of the perceived object—they would be equally external to the perceived object, and the generality of the reference to the causal efficacy of the perceived object would be *equally general* with respect to them. Again, the subjective condition of the perceiver would be as external to the causal efficacy of the perceived object as the external objective condition of the perceived object would be to the object. The *internal* condition of the perceived object—its causal efficacy with respect to the sense-data that constitute its perception—would be equally distinct from both of them.

This generality of the reference to the perceived object—a generality covering both the subjective condition of the perceiver and the external objective condition of the object—would preclude a perception of the object that would be independent of its effect (the First Consequence drawn from Grice's theory), since it would be independent of the subjective condition of the perceiver, and thus a logical connection between the two consequences would have been established independently of the previous argument supporting the idea of the same logical connection. For in order for the generality of the causal efficacy of the perceived object to be as independent of the subjective condition of the perceiver as it is of its own *external* objective condition, the perceived object could not be perceived as it performs its role in the causal origin of its perception, since its perception would causally depend on the subjective condition of the perceiver and in that role the perceived object *could not be perceived*, since in performing

2.8 Explanation of the Connection between the Two Consequences — 35

the role it would be causally independent of the subjective condition of the perceiver. Therefore, it could be perceived only through its effect (assuming that the argument remains within the framework of Grice's causal theory of perception). This is none other than the First Consequence of Grice's theory. Consequently, the Second Consequence entails the First Consequence. We have thus explained the connection between the two consequences of the theory in the general terms of the relation of cause and effect, and thus more generally than it was explained in the immediately preceding section of the chapter, and it therefore does so independently of the argument given in that section, since the generality of the reference to the causal efficacy of the perceived object in the present argument is not a generalization, or an abstraction, from the preceding argument, but is carried out in terms of just the concept of cause and effect.

The reliance on the cause-effect relation just given can be distinguished from an argument that relies instead on two distinctions: first, a broadly logical distinction between a *certain* object, following Strawson's use of "a certain object," or an object referred to through a *singular* term, on the one hand, and *whatever* object satisfies a certain general condition, or an object referred to through a *general* term, or a term in the predicative position in a predication, on the other hand; and second, an epistemological distinction between a reference to or knowledge of an object that is *a priori*, or independent of experience, on the one hand, and a reference to or knowledge of an object that is *a posteriori*, i.e. a reference or knowledge that depends on experience, and hence, perception, on the other hand. On the basis of these two distinctions we can proceed with the argument.

It could not be a *certain* object that would be logically required to play a role in the causal origin of a perception, if the object were to causally depend on *whatever* object would be necessary for it to play that role, since the causal connection that is included in the logical connection between the concept of a perception of a material object and the object can take only a *certain* object in the role of the cause of the sense-data (or experience) that constitute(s) the perception of the object (on Grice's causal theory of perception). But the putatively specified (i.e. *certain*) object's causal dependence on whatever object it would causally depend on would make it itself *whatever* object would be the causal consequence of this latter causal dependence, and thus keep the object from being the *certain* object required by Grice's theory to play its assigned role in the causal origin of the perception (denial of the Second Consequence of Grice's causal theory). Moreover, with regard to the second distinction under discussion, since it would be *whatever* object that would be the object in question, then if it were to be determined *which* object the object in question would be, it would have to be possible that it could be perceived independently of its effect, for that would be the only way to determine it, i.e. *a posteriori*, since its causal independence from its effect and the logical independence of its effect from it, would eliminate the possibility that the concept of the effect could determine the object, leaving only experience, and in particular, perception, to determine it, and that perception would be independent of the object's effect (denial of the First Consequence of Grice's causal theory).

2.9 The Two Consequences of Grice's Theory, the Single-object/Dual-Aspect Ontology Involved in the Theory, and Time

The perceived object is the object of the *ascription* of the property of being perceived; it is also the object the plays a logically required role in the *causal origin* of its being perceived. This is one of two consequences of a single-object /dual-aspect ontology (that was introduced in the last chapter) that are germane to our discussion. So, being perceived is a property that can be both *ascribed* to the object and the *effect* of the object. Since ascription is a logical and not a causal relation, and since effects cannot be ascribed to objects, at least not in the objects' causal role in question— cause and effect being a relation between logically distinct things, which keeps the effects from being properties that can be ascribed to their causes—being perceived is not ascribable to the object insofar as the object has the causal efficacy with respect to its being perceived, despite the fact that being perceived is ascribable to the same object that plays a role in the causal origin of its being perceived. This accounts for the First Consequence of Grice's theory in terms of the single-object/dual-aspect ontology, since that particular consequence states that the perceived object cannot be perceived independently of its effect.

On the other hand, the perceived object is the object the plays the logically required role in the causal origin of its being perceived; it is also the object of the ascription of the property of being perceived. So, the perceived object both plays a role in the *causal origin* of its being perceived and is the object of the *ascription* of the property of being perceived. However, if the object is the effect of or conditioned by *another* object, the property being ascribed to it—being perceived—would at least in part be the effect of or conditioned by the other object, an object that is not the perceived object. Hence, the perceived object would be the object of an ascription of a property that causally depends, not on just the perceived object itself, but on another object as well—an ascription of a property that would therefore not match the perceived object. This property need not be restricted to being perceived; it could be any property among a range of suitably ascribable properties. To prevent this discrepancy, the object cannot be allowed to be an effect of or conditioned by another object. This accounts for the Second Consequence of Grice's theory in terms of a single-object/dual-aspect ontology.

The last item to account for in terms of a single-object/dual-aspect ontology is the exclusion of time from the causal relation between the perceived object and its role in the causal origin of its perception, and therefore in the causal origin of the object's being perceived. Equivalently, it is the inclusion of the àtemporality of, or the subsumption under, the causal relation between the perceived object and its being perceived.

The immediately preceding section of this chapter argues that the causal efficacy of the perceived object with respect to the sense-data that constitute its perception can be referred to only *generally*, or in terms of logical *quantification*, where the notion of generality, or quantification, is contrasted with that of the *singularity* of the reference to the sense-data that constitute the object's perception, where the causal efficacy of the object with respect to the sense-data that constitute its perception could not itself be perceived through the sense-data, and therefore could not be perceived on Grice's causal theory of perception. Consequently, any statement that putatively refers to the causal efficacy of the perceived object with respect to the sense-data that constitute the object's perception would also be general, or quantified, as would therefore be a statement referring to any temporal relation between the sense-data and the object under the concept of cause and effect. However, since on Grice's causal theory of perception the sense-data that constitute a perception of the perceived object are referred to neither generally, or in terms of quantification, nor under the concept of cause and effect (i.e. constituents of the sense-data are not related to each other as cause and effect), no time in which they are related to each other would be a time in which they are related to the object on which they causally depend, i.e. the perceived object. Therefore, the causal relation between the sense-data and the perceived object would not be a relation in the same time in which the data are related to each other, and hence would not be a relation in the same time in which the data constitute a perception of the object.

More generally, there could be no determinate temporal causal relation *both* between the object and the sense-data that constitute a perception of the object *and* among the data themselves, if the data were temporally related to each other, since that would entail that the data be understood ambiguously, as standing in distinct temporal relations—one set belonging to their causal relation to the object and the other belonging to their relation to each other insofar as they constitute a perception of the object. Therefore, if the sense-data that constitute a perception of the object are related to each other in time, then either the causal relation of the data to the object is *not* a temporal relation at all *or* the data are not related to the object in the time in which they constitute a perception of the object. If the latter alternative is chosen—that there would be two distinct times involved—there would be an unavoidable ambiguity in our understanding the possibility that the object plays a role in the causal origin of the data *that constitute a perception of the object*, since distinct times would be involved in our understanding—one involving the object and the data and the other involving just the data. On the other hand, one way to avoid the alternative that the causal relation between the object and the data is àtemporal is to reject the condition that the data are temporally related to each other in terms in which they constitute a perception of the object. This would involve viewing the temporal relation they have to each other as belonging to the same time in which they are causally related to the object. But this way of avoiding the alternative in question only raises the question of how the sense-data can constitute a perception of the object on Grice's causal theory of perception. It would collapse his causal theory of perception into a theory involving an ordinary, physical causal relation between not only the object and the data, but among the data as well. It would then not be possible for Grice to argue that the causal relation between the object and the data is a *logically* necessary condition for the data to be a perception of the object. It would instead be only a condition that is causally necessary as ordinary conditions in general are causally necessary.

Finally, the connection between the single-object/dual aspect ontology and the arguments just given in support of the idea that the causal relation between the perceived object and the sense-data that constitute its perception lies in the remark just made. For, as already noted, if Grice were to hold that the causal relation between the object and the sense-data were temporal, it would be a general, or quantified, statement that the object and the data are causally related in time. However, as the last remark brings to our attention, if they are so related, the (temporal) causal relation would be ordinary or physical. But this would entail that Grice's ontology is really dual-object, not single-object, since the ontology of a theory of ordinary causal relations is dual-object. It is the *logical* connection between a perception and its object that contributes to the single-object nature of Grice's ontology—a logical connection that nonetheless includes the causal connection that gives the theory its name.

The above argument can be summarized in four steps. (1) The time in which a causal relation between two terms exists must be a time in which the terms are related to each other. (2) But the time in which there exists an object that can play a role in the causal origin of the sense-data that constitute a perception of the object cannot be the time in which the data are temporally related to each other. If the times involved were identical, the data would be only effects of the object and would not thereby constitute a perception of the object. (3) Therefore, no time in which the data that constitute a perception of an object that plays a role in the causal origin of the perception are correlated with each other can be a time in which the object exists. (4) Consequently, there can be no time in which there exists both the object and the data that constitute its perception, and hence there can be no time in which there exists the causal connection between the object and the data that constitute its perception.

Per contra, the last item to account for in a *dual-object* ontology is the *inclusion* of time, or temporality, in, or its *subsumption* under, the causal relation, or the concept of cause and effect, between the perceived object and its role in the causal origin of its perception, and therefore in the causal origin of the object's being perceived, but not perceived through the sense-data that constitute its perception. For the dual-object ontology entails that the perceived object may be *both* a temporal causal antecedent of its perception that exists in an ordinary causation, where the perception does not involve any sense-data as its constituents—and a temporal causal consequence of its own temporal causal antecedent. The perception that would not involve any sense-data as its constituents would be an effect of the perceived object in an ordinary causation in which the perceived object, and thus the ordinary causation, would therefore exist in time. The perception would not conform to a technical or philosophical theory of perception, which would involve the philosophical or technical term of *sense-data* that constitute the perception of the object. The dual-object ontology would thus entail *three* objects or conditions: the two *aspects* of the single-object/dual aspect ontology actually become two *objects*, and thus a dual-*object* ontology—the perceived object and its effect, which would be a perception of the object—iff the cause of the effect, that is, iff the perceived object, is also an effect of or conditioned by *another* object (the third object). This other object would be necessary if the perceived object were to be an effect (of the third object) as well as the cause of its own effect (its perception in an ordinary causation).

2.10 An Objection to 2.9. and a Reply

It may be objected that the identity of a perceived object that belongs to a single-object ontology may exist in time despite the conclusion of the section of this chapter just concluded, since the identity may be an identity over time—an *endurance* or a *continuant*[18]—such as the identity that belongs to the material objects that are obviously taken by Grice and Strawson as the perceived objects

---

18 On using a term of A. J. Ayer's, see P. F Strawson, *Skepticism and Naturalism: Some Varieties* (New York: Columbia University Press, 1983), p. 42, which cites Ayer's *The Central Questions of Philosophy*, chapter 5 (London: Widenfeld and Nicholson, 1973).

that constitute the domain of the proposed causal theory of perception. My reply is that the identity of such an enduring or "continuant" object entails that it *could* be perceived independently of its effect(s), including its perception, and that its causal efficacy with respect to its effect(s), i.e. its own perception, *could* be an effect of or conditioned by an external object.

The argument has several steps. First, if the endurance of the perceived object were not to be devoid of a principled explanation, the application of Grice's theory would entail a connection among the existences of the temporal stages of the object, that is, a causal connection: a later, causally consequential stage of the object would causally depend on an earlier, causally antecedent stage of the object, and so on to every earlier, causally antecedent stage. Second, any stage would therefore be the causally efficacious stage that it is because of the causal efficacy of its causally antecedent stage or stages. Third, the identification of any stage would therefore depend on either an identification of an antecedent stage, thereby starting an infinite regress, *or*, avoiding such a regress, simply identifying the stage in question. On Grice's causal theory of perception, an identification of the stage in question would be a perception of the object at that stage. Fourth, that perception would be independent of the effect of the object at that stage, which, *ex hypothesi*, would be an effect that would be a perception of the object. But, fifth, since Grice's theory *prohibits* such an independent perception of the object,[19] then either an infinite regress would be started and there would be no perception at all of the object regarding its causal efficacy with respect to its perception, or there would be a perception of the object, but the theory of the perception would not be Grice's causal theory, but would instead be a non-causal theory of perception. Consequently, identity over time would entail the denial of the First Consequence of Grice's causal theory of perception. Therefore, on his theory, the identity of the perceived object regarding its causal efficacy with respect to its perception could not be an identity over time.

An argument of the same form but with different terms can also be used to reply to the objection, if the possibility of the perceived object's being an effect of or conditioned by an external object or condition (the denial of the Second Consequence of Grice's theory) were substituted for the possibility of the same object's being perceived independently of its effect (the denial of the First Consequence of Grice's theory). The conclusion of 2.9. would be thus confirmed accordingly.

---

19 See 2.4. above.

3 Kant's Theory of Practical Causality

3.1 Transition from Grice to Kant

Grice's causal theory of perception faced a certain problem about the perceived object's *causal efficacy regarding the sense-data that constitute its perception* (henceforth abbreviated as CESDP). The problem stemmed from the apparent possibility that that causal efficacy in turn causally depended on the causal efficacy of another object. Since the sense-data would not be what they would have been had the perceived object been self-sufficient in it role in the production of the data, and since the data constituted its perception, the efficacy of the *other* object would *confound* the data, and thus confound the perception of the perceived object, since the data would be an effect of both the perceived object and the other object, and yet the perception would purportedly be a perception of just the perceived object. In a word, the data would no longer *match* the perceived object—there would be a *mismatch* or a *discrepancy* between the data and the perceived object. And if there were such a discrepancy, there would be a *division* between the *ascription* of the perception to the object and the *causal attribution* of the perception to the object other than the perceived object as well as to the perceived object.

The non-modal indirect argument offered in support of the same conclusion was that *ex hypothesi* "the other object has a causal effect on the perceived object's causal efficacy with respect to the sense-data that constitute [its perception]. If the other object's effect on the perceived object made *no* difference to the data, and hence no difference in the perception of the perceived object, it would fall outside the reach of Grice's causal theory of perception." Since it does make such a difference, the perception reflects the difference, which confounds the perception, since the perception, on the causal theory, is supposed to be a perception of just the perceived object, and not another object, an object on which the perceived object causally depends for its CESDP. The distinction between being perceived through sense-data and playing a role in the causal origin of the data creates the possibility of a confounding of the perception between the perceived object and another object that also is causally involved in the sense-data that constitute the perception. To eliminate the possibility of such confounding, that is, to assure that the perception would be singularly objective, or objectively undivided, in its reference to the perceived object—to assure a *match* between the data, and hence the perception, and the perceived object—it was concluded that at least either of two steps had to be taken. One was to exclude the perceived object's causal dependence on another object for its CESDP. Both Grice and Strawson tried to take this step, but Grice's was unsuccessful because of its circularity, and Strawson took it by *specifying* the perceived object from the start rather than relying on the mode in which the perceived object brings about the sense-data that constitute its perception, as Grice tried to do.

The other step was to switch the theory of perception from a causal theory to a non-causal one. After all, it was the causal theory that raised the question of whether another object could confound the perception of the perceived object, since it was the causal theory that excluded the possibility of a perception of the object that would be independent of the object's effects (the First Consequence of Grice's causal theory). This led to the reasoning that, if the perceived object *were* affected by another object with respect to perceived object's causal efficacy regarding the perceived object's effect(s), and since the perceived object's perception would be such an effect, the other object, since it influenced the CESDP, would influence the perception of the perceived object, thereby confounding the perception, since two distinct objects would be causally involved in the same perception, which purportedly would be singular in its reference to the perceived object.

On the other hand, if the perception conformed to a *non-causal* theory of perception, it could not be confounded by an object other than the perceived object, since it could not be confounded by any object through its causal dependence on the object, for the simple reason that the perception would not causally depend on *any* object, its being a perception that would conform to a *non-causal* theory of perception. Consequently, the causal efficacy of the perceived object with respect to its effect (which can no longer be the object's perception through the object's CESDP) *can* causally depend on another object without confounding its perception. However, this switch to a non-causal theory of perception of the object insofar as the object stands between its causal antecedent (the "other" object) and its causal consequent, i.e. its own effect, allows the effect to be a perception, but does not require it, and it even allows the effect to be a perception of the perceived object, but, again, does not require it, as would be required by Grice's causal theory of perception. Thus, on a non-causal theory, a possible perception of the perceived object could be an effect of the perceived object whose causal efficacy would itself be causally dependent on another object, but without the causal dependence's confounding the perception, since the other object could not affect the sense-data that constitute the perception of the object that is perceived non-causally. To sum up, one solution to the problem of confounding a perception of an object that was presented by the perceived object's causal dependence on another object in the respect in question was for the causal theory of perception somehow to *exclude* the causal dependence on another object in that respect; the other solution was to *keep* the causal dependence on another object, but to switch the theory of perception from a causal to a non-causal one. The switch would entail a switch in type of causation, from a causation in perception to an ordinary causation.

The transition from Grice's causal theory of perception to Kant's causal theory of action starts with our concern with the effects of other objects on the perceived object's causal efficacy with respect to its own effects, as dealt with according to Grice's theory, so with Kant we are also concerned with what Kant considers *external* conditions on the will that affect *its* effects, i.e. its actions, and these would be *empirical* conditions on the will, since their being external entails for Kant their involving feeling (*Gefühl*) or sensation (*Empfindung*). Like the perceived object in our discussion of Grice that causally depends on an object other than the perceived object with respect to the latters' causal efficacy regarding its own effect, empirical conditions on the will, as has already been evident in our discussion of Kant, in affecting the causal efficacy of the will with respect to its actions affect the *effects* of the will, i.e. its actions. In both cases, the causal efficacy of the object in question—the perceived object for Grice and the will for Kant—*cannot be allowed to be an effect of or conditioned by another object*, lest the other object, that is, the *external* object, affect the effect of the perceived object or of the will, thereby confounding the perception or the action that results, respectively. The causal efficacy of the perceived object or of the will with respect to its perception or its action must therefore be independent, or free, of any external object that would have an effect on the effect of the perceived object or the will. Thus on our interpretation of Grice and on Kant's own explicit statement of what he calls the "negative" sense of the causal efficacy of objects of reason, the causal efficacy of the object in question—whether the perceived object or the will—with respect to its effect that is relevant to our discussion must be independent of the causal efficacy of every *external* object. It was precisely the recognition of this property of freedom from the causal efficacy of every external object that is shared by Grice's perceived object and Kant's will that, incidentally, started my work on the idea that Kant's theory of the freedom of the will could be found like a palimpsest beneath Grice's causal theory of perception.

To draw the relation between the respective *causal* theories of Kant and Grice even closer, both would hold, on my interpretation of each, that in every case in which an external object has an effect on the causal efficacy of a given object or subject—the perceived object or the will—with respect to *its* effect, that is, its perception or its action, either of the two steps described above must be taken, if confounding of the perception or the action is to be avoided. *Either* the causal theory excludes the possibility of any effect of an external object on the causal efficacy of perceived object or the will with respect to its own effects *or* the philosopher switches from the causal theory of perception or of action to a non-causal theory. With respect to the latter step, the perceived object or the will would no longer be considered to play a role in the *causal* origin of the perception or the action, but of course it would still be considered to play a role in the causal origin of its *effect*, which obviously could not be its perception or its action as that would be viewed from the standpoint of Grice's causal theory of perception or Kant's causal theory of action. This philosophical switch from a causal to a non-causal theory is one of the two ways mentioned above to keep Grice's perception from being confounded by an external object, and it also would keep Kant's action from being confounded by an effect of an external object on the causal efficacy of the will with respect to the action. So, for both Grice's causal theory of perception and Kant's causal theory of action, the switch from a causal to a non-causal theory protects the causal theory from intrusions into the objectivity and singularity of Grice's perception—the singularity in its referential relation to its object—on the one hand, and, on the other, it protects Kant's causal theory of action from external intrusions into the causality of the will with respect to its actions.

One last preliminary refinement—an all-important one—is necessary before we turn to the application of Kant's causal theory of action to any actual case in which the will plays a role in the causal origin of an action. So far in these preliminaries we have spoken of the confounding of only the perception or the action that would be due to the influence of an external object or condition on the perceived object's or the will's causal efficacy regarding its *perception* or its *action*, and therefore of the need to exclude the influence of an external object or condition. But we have already seen that the problem is not quite that, but is really deeper than that: it is that since the sense-data that constitute the perception in Grice's causal theory of perception or, the corresponding term in Kant's causal theory of action, viz., the *maxim* that constitutes the action, causally depend(s) on the perceived object or on the will, the effect on an external object or condition on the perceived object's or the will's causal efficacy with respect to the sense-data or the maxim that constitutes the perception or the action would affect the very sense-data or the maxim that constitutes the perception or the action. The aforementioned "all-important" point is that it is only the effect of an external object on precisely the sense-data or the maxim that constitutes the perception or the action that is the real problem of the interference of an external object with the causal efficacy of the perceived object or of the will. Apart from the sense-data or the maxim constituting a perception of an object or an action of the will, there would be no theoretical need or even plausibility to exclude the influence of any external object on the perceived object's or the will's causal efficacy with respect to the perception of the perceived object or the action of the will. Any such attempt, because it would be unnecessary, would only be obfuscating.[1] Indeed, what started Grice's search for a way to isolate the per-

---

[1] To borrow an idea from Strawson; P. F. Strawson, "Causation in Perception," in *Freedom and Resentment and Other Essays* (London and New York: Routledge, 2008, first published, Methuen & Co Ltd., 1974), p. 83.

ceived object from other objects that are also causally required by a perception, such as light and the perceiver's requisite senses, a search started by the problems with the causal theory of perception that were introduced into the relatively recent literature by H. H. Price,[2] was the very acknowledgement that any of these external objects could enable or disable any perceived object's causal efficacy with respect to its perception. Material objects cannot be seen in the dark, for example, nor can they be seen if the perceiver's senses are not functioning adequately. Consequently, external objects such as light and adequate senses cannot be plausibly excluded in any ordinary account of perception or Kant's naturalistic account of action. But they must be excluded by a causal theory of perception, such as Grice's, or of action, such as Kant's, that takes a perception or an action to consist of sense-data or a maxim, since such *ordinary* causal factors as light and the adequacy of the perceiver's senses can have nothing causal to do with the sense-data that *theoretically* causally depend on both the subjective conditions of the perceiver and the perceived object, nor can any *ordinary* empirical condition of the will have anything causal to do with the maxim of an action that *theoretically* causally depends on both the subjective, or external, and the objective, or internal, conditions of the will. This entails that any such external object or condition that would belong to what Grice calls an *ordinary causation* and what Kant calls a *natural* causation can have no effect whatsoever on the sense-data or the maxim that constitute a perception or an action and belong to the respective causal theories involved. Relative to ordinary (Grice) or natural (Kant) causations, sense-data and maxims are theoretical entities, or as some would or used to say "hypothetical constructs," of causal theories of perception and action, respectively, constituting their respective material content, and ordinary external objects cannot affect that content: only the subjective conditions of the perceiver or of the will and the objective conditions of the perceived object or, again, the will, can affect it, and thereby have an effect on it. If an external object or condition is to affect the material content of a perception or an action, it must affect the perceiver or the will, and in so doing become a subjective condition of the perceiver or the will. As such a condition, it does affect the content.

To recapitulate the adaptation of Kant to Grice, Kant's *maxim* that constitutes an action shares with Grice's key feature of *sense-data* that constitute a perception a dependence on the subject involved in the action or the perception, that is, their respective *subjectivity*. And Kant's causal theory of action further shares with Grice's causal theory of perception the feature that this *subjectivity* of the maxim and of the sense-data that constitute(s) an action and a perception, respectively, is the feature that the action and the perception can be ascribed to

---

[2] H. H. Price, *Perception* (London: Methuen & Co. Ltd., 1954, first published, 1932), pp. 69–70.

the will of the agent and the perceived object—their respective *objectivity—only if the action and the perception, respectively, causally depend on the will of the agent and the perceived object*. Thus, a subjective maxim or sense-data constitute an objective action or perception only if the will of an agent or the perceived object is causally involved in the maxim's constituting an action of the will of an agent or the sense-data's constituting a perception of the object. Since sense-data or a maxim constitute a perception or an action of an object or the will, respectively, only if the object or the will produces the data (on Grice's causal theory of perception or Kant's causal theory of action), no other object or faculty of a subject can *possibly* produce the data or the maxim that constitute the perception of (just) the object or the action of (just) the will. So, on either Grice's or Kant's causal theory of perception or action, the perceived object or the will cannot be an effect of or conditioned by another object with respect to the perceived object's CESDP or the will's causal efficacy regarding the maxim of an action. The perceived object or the will uniquely satisfies the causal requirement of the respective theory: the theory entails the unique satisfaction of the causal requirement, since the theory holds that it is the causal involvement of the perceived object or the will that makes the sense-data a perception of the object or a maxim the maxim of an action.

In summary of these preliminaries, it is the will's role in the causal origin of what in our interpretation of Kant's causal theory of action that corresponds to Grice's sense-data that constitute a perception of the object, viz., Kant's maxim of an action, that will be our primary concern in the discussion that follows. But since, still following Grice, we will be contrasting Kant's causal theory of action with his non-causal theory of action, just as with Grice we contrasted his causal theory of perception with what we called a non-causal theory of perception, our logically related concern will be with what will be called Kant's *non-causal theory of action*, where the maxim of an action still plays a necessary role in the theory—a role through which an action can be ascribed to the will—but where *it does not causally depend on the will*, and thus would be independent of any external object or condition that affects the will with respect to the will's role in the specifically causal origin of its effect.

3.2 Application of Kant's Causal Theory of Action: Kant's *Incompatibilism*

Following the adaptation to Grice's causal theory of perception that was employed for the application of causal theories to the cases of memory, writing a history of an event, direct reference, which was patterned after Strawson's adaptation, and applying it to Quinean meaning as well–all in the last chapter—we will now apply it to Kant's causal theory of action.

To review briefly, a *maxim* for Kant is the principle on which the subject acts and is viewed by her as valid only for her will, in contradistinction with a *practical law*, which is known as valid for "every rational being," i.e. for everyone. Through her will she enacts her maxim, puts it into action, or activates it; that is, her will plays a necessary role in the causal origin of the action that is constituted, determined, or described, by the maxim, or more specifically, by the determinations of the maxim, and thus of the action consisting of the maxim. An example Kant considers at the start of KvP is that of a "pathologically affected will" of a person who makes it her maxim to take revenge at every affront. ("pathologically affected" here and elsewhere in KvP means that the will is affected by an object or condition that is *external* to the will, in the sense of "external" already employed—a sense that it is a condition that, as Kant also says, "attaches to the will contingently.") This maxim could take the Gricean-style form of *its seeming to the agent as if she were taking revenge at her being affronted*. If the agent's will were to put this maxim into action, it would be impossible for her will to be *conditioned* by her inclination to take revenge at every affront, since her maxim would constitute her action—the *effect* of her will—and therefore her will could not be conditioned by it. In general, it is impossible for a condition to play a role in the causal origin of its own existence, including a case in which it belongs to an effect of the condition, such as the case of revenge presently under discussion. That is, the agent is taking revenge at being affronted; she did not just take revenge, or even do it "for its own sake," whatever sense that may make. Hence, being affronted could not activate or otherwise condition or influence her will in a role in the causal origin of the existence of the revenge, since it belongs to the maxim of her action, which is the existence of the revenge. Moreover, the same would hold for any *external* condition of the will, whether it is an inclination, a sensible incentive that is contained in a maxim, or the activation of such. But, since the moral law can itself be an incentive of the will as a direct influence on the will to take an action and since the law is *internal* to the will, then, since the ground of the law would be pure practical reason, it could not be limited in its influence on the will in the way that an inclination or a sensible incentive of the will could be limited, since they would be limited by the very feeling of respect for the moral law, whereas the law would be the *origin* of that feeling. In any case, that is what Kant asserts in order to ascribe to the will a purely rational and intellectual incentive (that is nonetheless felt) to take action for the sake of the law, i.e. to act out of duty. In other words, the moral law would be a merely "formal limiting" condition on the will, since it would only be limiting itself—its limitation being a consequence of the mere form of the structure of the terms involved.

The foregoing reasoning employed the principle that if the maxim of an action makes an external condition of the will part of the action, then, since the action causally depends on the will, the condition cannot be a condition of the will in the will's role in the causal origin of the action. Every external condition of the will thus puts a constraint on every maxim: the condition could not belong to the maxim. But this would have the disastrous entailment for Kant's ethical theory (which must allow for the possibility of immoral action) that the agent could not do anything about any external condition of her will —an entailment Henry Sidgwick apparently drew from his reading of Kant which we discussed earlier.[3] She could not, for example, adopt the maxim to take revenge at every affront. On the other hand, she could only adopt a maxim to take an action that would give her moral credit, such as morally check her temptation to keep for herself money left with her for safekeeping by a late friend who left no record of the deposit. Since on Kant's notion of a maxim of an immoral action, it must contain an external condition of the will as an incentive of the will, either the immoral maxim would be impossible or the causal efficacy of the will regarding the action determined or described by the maxim would be impossible.[4] Since every human action covered by Kant's causal or non-causal theory of action is determined or described by the maxim chosen by the agent, that is, unless the action is conceived to be the result of a *natural*, or in Grice's terms, *ordinary*, causation, to avoid this disastrous entailment, it follows that his causal theory of action entails that *no external condition of the will can affect the will in its role in the causal origin of an action*. This is none other than a statement of Kant's negative sense of noumenal freedom, and it corresponds so precisely with the Second Consequence that we previously derived from Grice's causal theory of perception that we can look forward to concluding a major objective of the book, viz., that, at least thus far in our investigation, Kant's causal theory of action can be fairly adapted to Grice's causal theory of perception in the respect just described.

---

[3] But see 5.1. below for a detailed discussion of Sidgwick.
[4] See Allison's "Incorporation Thesis"; Allison's problem is that he takes the maxim of an action to be part of the rational agency for putting the maxim into action; rather, the maxim belongs to the effect of the rational agency, not part of the agency itself

3.3 Application of Kant's Non-causal Theory of Action: His *Compatibilism*

On the other hand, an action can be ascribed to the will through its maxim according to Kant's *non-causal* theory of action, whether the incentive in the maxim is based on an external or internal condition of the will, since *ex hypothesi* the maxim would be causally independent of the will. Kant's non-causal theory of action would thus be adapted to the non-causal theory of perception described in the previous chapter. It would make it possible for the will to be empirically identified through an action that can be ascribed to it independently of any empirical identification through its *effect*. For example, on Kant's non-causal theory of action, revenge that could be ascribed to the will through the maxim to take revenge at every affront could empirically identify the will independently of the will's effect(s), since on his *non-causal* theory, revenge that is constituted through its maxim and can thereby be ascribed to the will is simply not an *effect* of the will. In such a non-causal relation between the will and revenge, the will is so affected by an affront that it exemplifies the maxim, but the revenge that is ascribed to the will does not causally depend on it, since no law causally connects the will and the revenge. However, revenge might be the causal consequence of an affront that prompts, or activates, the *inclination* of the will to take revenge at every affront—revenge that causally depends on the will, but could not be ascribed to it through the *maxim* to take revenge at every affront. In such a case, the causal dependence would be *natural*. Hence, on Kant's non-causal theory of action, revenge could, at an affront to the agent, be ascribed, but not causally attributed, to the will through the *maxim* to take revenge at every affront, whereas revenge could, again at an affront to the agent, be causally attributed, but not ascribed, to the will through the *inclination* to take revenge at every affront, but independently of the maxim that is described by the description of the inclination. In the latter instance, the action, the will, the inclination, and its prompting, or activation, by the affront, would all be part of a causation that would be considered by Kant as *natural* and by Grice as *ordinary*. The *maxim* of the action would play no role in such a causation, although it would play a role in the ascription of the action to the will in its role in the causation, and hence would play a role in the empirical identification of the will.

To make the conclusion even more comprehensive, revenge that could be ascribed, but not causally attributed, to the will on a *non-causal theory of action*, could also be causally attributed, but not ascribed, to the will *in the absence of any theory of action that entails a maxim of the action*, where the action would therefore be the effect in a *natural causation*, and, moreover, where the action could also be ascribed to the will to which it could be *causally* attributed on Kant's *causal theory of action*. We would thus need to distinguish between Kant's causal and his non-causal theories of action, both of which involve the maxim of an action, and his naturalistic theory of action, where the causal connection, or the causal law, between the will and an action is natural, but where the idea of a maxim of an action has no role to play in the theory. Finally, between Kant's causal and non-causal theories of action, only the non-causal theory is compatible with his naturalistic theory of action, since it is an account of how a maxim can be constitutive of an action (revenge) that can, through the maxim, be ascribed to a will that brings about an action (revenge) because of —and here is Kant's naturalistic theory of action—an external condition of the will (an inclination to take revenge at every affront) that is prompted, or activated, by an external object (an affront to the agent).

There is no need to throw up our hands in frustration at failing to find a unique solution to the question of how to view the respective roles of the will, the action, the maxim, the inclination, and the activation of the maxim or the inclination. There is no unique solution because there is no unique view of the role the elements can play in Kant's perhaps dizzying array of theories. For example, on his *non-causal* theory of action, the action of vengeance at an affront can be ascribed to a will through the aforementioned maxim (to seek vengeance at every affront) but cannot be causally attributed to the will, since the theory of the action is *non-causal*; on another view, however, but still viewed according to Kant's non-causal theory of action, but where the causation is natural, the vengeance *can* be causally attributed to the will, since it would be an effect of the will, but it cannot be ascribed to the will through the aforementioned maxim, since a maxim plays no role in a natural causation. Of course, the vengeance can empirically identify the will in its role in the natural causation and, moreover, identify it independently of its effect, without the action itself playing a role in the causation (since it consists of its maxim). On the first view of the vengeance, again, viewed from the standpoint of Kant's *non-causal* theory of action, the affront would condition the will in its role as the subject of the ascription of the vengeance, but not as the subject of a causal attribution of the vengeance, since on this view of the vengeance the will would not be the subject of a causal attribution of the vengeance. The opposite, of course, would obtain on the other view of the vengeance: there the affront would condition the will as the subject of the causal attribution of the vengeance, but not as the subject of the ascription of the vengeance. Independently of the just mentioned two-fold views of the elements involved, there is Kant's two-fold view of the action— the vengeance: the causal and the non-causal theories of the action. Kant's causal theory of the vengeance would be *incompatible* with any *causal* dependence on an external condition—the inclination or the affront—the will might otherwise have with respect to its own causal efficacy regarding its action—the revenge—whereas his non-causal theory of the vengeance would be fully compatible with the will's natural causal dependence on the inclination and the affront in its bringing about the vengeance. One way of distinguishing between Kant's two theories of action is that on the causal theory, the will plays a role in the causal origin of the action through its activation of the maxim that constitutes the action, but it does so independently of every external condition of the will, whereas on the non-causal theory of the action, the will does play a role in the causal origin of an action through its causal dependence on an external condition of the will, but, to reiterate an important point made earlier, it does so independently of its own prompting, or activation, of the maxim that constitutes the action that is ascribed to it (the prompting, or activation, would be due to an external condition of the will, such as an affront, in case the action is vengeance at an affront) and independently of the maxim that would constitute the action on either theory of action—whether causal or non-causal.

3.4 The Three Alternative Views and the Texts

The three alternative views of the elements are amply exemplified by the texts. With regard to Kant's non-causal theory of action, he often speaks of actions whose antecedents are not causal. There are, for example, actions that are taken by the will according to hypothetical imperatives, where the necessity of the rule that leads to the action is conditional on an object of the will that is of interest only to the agent. In that case, the will does not play a role in any *causal* origin of the action, since the necessity of the rule determining the agent's conduct depends on the end, or object, of the action, which in turn depends on the condition of the agent—an external condition of her will, and the variability of the application of the rule keeps its necessity from being unconditional; yet unconditional necessity is essential to any rule that is a law, and law is essential to causality, or more specifically, efficient causality. Such would be the case if the agent were rational about choosing vengeance in response to an affront. Apart from hypothetical imperatives and the choice of a rationally but nonetheless conditionally necessary means to an end, Kant speaks of *general determinations of the will* that fall short of being contained even in hypothetical imperatives, but which are contained in maxims whose rules the agent would view as valid for herself alone, as our foregoing discussion of an agent's maxim to take revenge at every affront has already made clear. That was a discussion of just the relation of the will to an action that was described by a maxim, without any implication of a causal connection between the will and the action. It allowed into our discussion the introduction of a non-causal, or ascription, theory according to which an action could be ascribed to the will without the implication that it could be causally attributed to the will. And the non-casual theory in turn allowed the will to be externally conditioned to play a role in the origin of an action that could be only causally attributed to the will, but not ascribed to it through any maxim of the action, and a role, furthermore, that would be distinct from its role in the causal origin of an action that could be only ascribed to it through a maxim that constituted the action, as viewed from the standpoint of Kant's causal theory of action. This would be its role in a naturalistic theory of the causal relation between the will and an action. Altogether, Kant's approach is a *contextualist* approach to the elements that can be said to exist in the relations that are comprehended in his conception of action as variously viewed from the three alternative standpoints.[5]

3.5 Recent Views About Kant on Rational Agency

Certain prominent Kant scholars would contest one of the major propositions that has just been asserted, viz., my claim that for Kant the activation of a maxim of an action cannot causally depend on an external condition of the will. Up to a certain point, however, they would agree with it, but thereafter the disagreement would be fundamental. We would all start in agreement with Henry Allison's recognition that every maxim of an action contains—Allison would say "incorporates"—an external condition of the will, among which Kant's *incentives* figure prominently in Allison's account.[6] He continues by distinguishing Kant's incompatibilism—the doctrine of the incompatibility between the spontaneity or freedom of the will or of choice with respect to the causal origin of actions and the determinism of the laws of nature regarding all cause and effect relations among events—from the compatibilism of Leibniz and Hume.[7] Allison and those who agree with him on this matter assert that for Kant incorporation of external conditions into a maxim entails the aforementioned spontaneity or freedom to make a rule of conduct one's maxim of action. Leibniz and Hume for their part, Allison says, give a naturalistic account of the causation of human action, leaving out the crucial spontaneity that sets Kant's theory of action apart from theirs.

---

5 For further discussion of these same points from 3.1.–3.4., but especially 3.4., see 7.5–7.8. below.
6 Henry E. Allison, *Kant's Theory of Freedom* (Cambridge, UK: Cambridge University Press, 1990), pp. 5–6, 39–40.
7 Allison, *Theory of Freedom*, pp. 5, 30.

But immediately after our agreement with Allison and those who follow his lead that every maxim for Kant contains of an external condition of the will, the fundamental disagreement between us begins. Where Allison and those on his side of the dispute[8] locate a maxim in Kant's theory of the *causal efficacy* of the will with respect to action and thus in his theory of *rational agency*, I have argued that their interpretation would make it impossible for an agent to do anything about any external condition of her will, such as her desire for pleasure, since as part of the *cause* of an action, an external condition cannot be part of the action that is the *effect*. It would make action useless for the pursuit of pleasure and the avoidance of pain, which everyone desires and avoids, respectively, since any maxim that contained that end or object would, on their interpretation, be part of Kant's theory of rational agency, or the causal *origin* of the action, and therefore not constitutive of its *effect*, i.e. the action itself, as I contend it must be according to Kant's causal theory of action. So, the opposition between their view and mine of Kant's theory of the causal efficacy of the will and an action is quite fundamental. The following passages from their writing should help make it clear that they include Kant's maxims as part of his theory of the causal efficacy of the will regarding its actions instead of their being determinations or descriptions of its effects, i.e. its actions, which is my view of where they belong.[9]

Henry Allison: "…incentives (*Triebfedern*) do not motivate by themselves causing action but rather by being taken as reasons and incorporated into maxims … the act of incorporation is conceived as the genuine causal factor."[10]

Allen Wood: "In the case of a will (or *free* power of choice), an empirical impulse does not act directly or mechanically as the cause of ac-

---

[8] See, for example, Allen W. Wood, *Kant's Ethical Thought* (Cambridge, UK: Cambridge University Press, 1999), pp, 51–2; Andrews Reath, *Agency and Autonomy: Kant's Moral Theory* (Oxford, UK, New York: Oxford University Press, 2006), pp. 12–3.

[9] My view agrees, but only up to a point, with Stephen Engstrom's: "Since the will is a causal power, its form can be described as a *law*, and in particular as a *practical law* . . ." *The Form of Practical Knowledge: A Study of the Categorical Imperative* (Cambridge, Mass., Harvard University Press, 2009), p. 134. Unlike the view of Henry Allison, Allen Wood, and Andrews Reath, the maxim of an action would belong to the agency of the will *only* in regard to their "universality that extends to all practical subjects" p.136. Since my claim, that the maxim of an action belongs instead to the *effect* of such agency, presumes, now contrary to Engstrom's view of the nature of maxims in general, that a maxim is viewed by the agent as valid only for herself, and not universally, I would otherwise be in agreement with him, and in disagreement with Allison *et al.*, with respect to the view of the role of maxims regarding the will's agency, viz., that they determine only the *effect* of the will, i.e. its action, and not its causal efficacy with respect to its action.

[10] Allison, *Theory of Freedom*, p. 51.

tion but serves instead only as an incentive (*Triebfeder*) to the adoption of a *principle* and the setting of an end. 'An incentive can determine the will to action *only insofar as the individual has taken it up into his maxim* (has made it into a general rule, according to which he will conduct himself' ([Kant,] *Religion within the boundaries of mere reason* 6:24). (This crucial Kantian idea has been emphasized by Henry Allison under the name "the Incorporation Thesis.")[11]

Andrews Reath: "Kant claims ...that an incentive never determines the will directly, but only through a spontaneous judgment or choice made by the individual that can be expressed as the adoption of a maxim. This conception of free agency ...indicates that Kant's conception of choice ...allow[s] an incentive to have an affective force of some sort, but the role assigned to such force in motivation and the explanation of action must be limited so as to leave room for the notion of choice."[12]

3.6 Rejection of Recent Views

On my view, however, there is a connection between the subjectivity of the sense-data (Grice) or the maxim (Kant) and the causal efficacy of only the perceived object (Grice) or the will of the agent (Kant), but not any other object or condition, with respect to the sense-data constituting a perception of the object (Grice) or the maxim constituting an action of the will of the agent (Kant). That is, the causal efficacy of another object or condition besides the perceived object or the will of the agent with respect to the sense-data that constitutes a perception of the perceived object or the maxim that constitutes an action of the will of the agent breaks the causal connection between the perceived object or the will of the agent and the sense-data that constitutes a perception of the object or the maxim that constitutes an action of the will of the subject such that it *confounds* the resulting perception of the perceived object or the resulting action of the will of the agent as understood according to Grice's causal theory of perception or Kant's causal theory of action. In brief, only the perceived object or the will of the agent has the causal connection with the sense-data that constitutes a perception of the object or the maxim that constitutes an action of the will of the agent that Grice's causal theory of perception

---

[11] Wood, *Kant's Ethical Thought*, p. 51.
[12] Reath, *Agency and Autonomy*, pp. 12–3.

or Kant's causal theory of action require, respectively, for the sense-data to constitute a perception of the perceived object or for the maxim to constitute an action of the will of the agent. With this causal theory of Kant's maxim as constituting an action of the will of an agent modeled after Grice's causal theory of sense-data as constituting a perception of an object, we can apply it to a particular case actually dealt with by Kant.

3.7 Grice's and Kant's Causal Theories and Time

As with so much of my interpretation of Kant's theory of action as a causal theory, its inclusion of time depends on my interpretation of the inclusion of time in Grice's causal theory of perception in 2.9. Use of the notion of *generality*, or *quantification*, of that interpretation will be evident in the argument that follows, which uses, not the correlative notion of singularity, and its companion notion of *immediacy*, which were previously employed to capture Grice's idea that *sense-data* are valid for the subject, or perceiver, alone, but Kant's closely related notion of the *subjectivity* of the maxim of an action of the will of the individual agent who is causally involved. Just as *sense-data* (and *experience*, for Strawson) is Grice's (and Strawson's, vis a vis *experience*) required term for the *direct*, i.e. *immediate*, relation between a perception and its object (as explained in the previous chapter, both Grice and Strawson hold that perception is imbued with thought through a concept)—a relation without the need of the *mediation* of a thought through a concept, if a mental state is to refer to an *existing* object—so Kant's *maxim* of an action is his required term for the direct, i.e. immediate, reference of an action to the free will of an *existing* agent, to whom the action can be ascribed iff the free will of the agent is causally necessary.

If *both* the relation between the free will and an action, on the one hand, *and* the relations among the determinations of the maxim of the action, which therefore constitute the action, on the other, exist in time, then, if the frameworks of the times in which the two sets of temporal relations exist, respectively, were different, we could not understand what the relation might be between the temporal relation between the existence of the will and that of the determinations of a maxim in an action, on the one hand, and the temporal relations among the determinations constituting the maxim, and hence the action, on the other. Yet without an understanding of such a relation between the two sets of temporal relations, we could not understand the role of the will in the causal origin of an action that comprises determinations of the will that are temporally related to each other. Their temporal relations to each other would count for nothing.

If, in order to avoid that result, we seek an identical time in which determinations of the will can be temporally related both to their causal origin in the will and to each other, then, of the two sets of times that seem possible in this connection, the framework of time that interrelates only the determinations of the will would *not* also interrelate the same determinations with the causality of the will. Therefore, if any framework of time would temporally interrelate *both* the will and its determinations *and* the determinations with each other, it could only be the framework of time, or simply, *the time*, in which the determinations are causally involved with the will. If that were the required identical time, however, since it would be a time in which the temporal relations among the determinations of an action would be valid or obtain regardless of the identity of the agent actually involved, and hence, regardless of the existence of the or any agent, it could *not* be a time in which the temporal relations among the determinations of an action belonged to the *maxim* of the action. Thus, the maxim, being valid only for the individual agent actually involved, would have no logical role to play, if the time in which the determinations of the action were temporally related to each other were the time of the causality of the will with respect to the determinations. Since no other time could be the identical time in which *both* the will played a causal role in the origin of an action *and* the determinations of the action could be temporally interrelated, no time could be such a time that the will plays a role in the causal origin of an action comprising the determinations that constitute the *maxim* of the action. In a word, the causal relation would have to be *timeless*. The àtemporality of the causality of the will, and thus the possibility of its freedom, is necessary if free will is to play its role in the causal origin of an action whose determinations are comprised by what, on this interpretation of free will, is essential to the action, viz., its maxim. Since the maxim, connoting utter subjectivity, is Kant's notion in his practical philosophy of the required existence of the subject, or agent, who is causally involved in an action subject to moral judgment, we conclude that for Kant the applicability or use of moral judgment with respect to an action—a use that can apply the utterly *general* or *objective* moral *law*, i.e. the Categorical Imperative—only to the just as utterly *singular* or *subjective* maxim of the action. This is the *critique* of practical pure reason that is the companion to the *critique* of theoretical pure *reason*, which restricts the application of the categories of the understanding to appearances—the corresponding utterly subjective objects of theoretical knowledge. In sum, completely general and objective representations for Kant can be applied only to completely singular and subjective ones. Such a dialectical complementarity seems to pervade both his theoretical and his practical thought.

4 Conscience: Remembering One's Forbidden Actions

"reason ... acknowledges no distinction of time ... but always connects the same sensation [viz., pain] with [the deed] morally, whether the deed is being done now or was done long ago" (KpV 5:99).

4.1 Another Way to Derive the Timelessness of the Causality of the Freedom of the Will

The epigram just above, which asserts the timelessness of an *action* produced by the freedom of the will, is employed by Kant to support the theory of transcendental idealism that entailed the timelessness of *the freedom of the will itself*, the idealism that Allen Wood condemned as a "desperate expedient"—a condemnation to which I took exception at the beginning of the Preface to the book. I return to the theory and to Wood's condemnation of it in order to use the epigram for my own purposes to support the grounds for the timelessness of free will that I am attributing to Kant —grounds for, and hence a theory of, the àtemporal causality of free will that is an alternative to the grounds that Kant himself proposes in the third Antinomy in the *Critique of Pure Reason* and to which Wood takes exception and which Kant more briefly again proposes in the *Critique of Practical Reason* (KpV 5:97–99), the textual origin of the epigram. Those idealistic grounds, which Kant states twice, support Kant's claim that the putative àtemporal causality of free will is the àtemporal causal antecedent of the *"empirical character"* of the agent, which is the immediate factor that leads directly to the agent's causal responsibility for her actions. The alternative ground I have proposed on Kant's behalf in the preceding chapters, out of recognition of contemporary criticism of his transcendental idealism, has been that the àtemporality of the causality of free will can be derived from Kant's concept of an *action* that is subject to moral judgment. That concept—and its causal theory of action—entails that only the àtemporal causality of free will can causally account for the enactment of a maxim in an action. The analysis or argument for the entailment was given in 3.7.

Briefly, the argument is that there could be no consistent set of temporal relations that *both* temporally interrelates just the determinations of the maxim of an action *and* also interrelates the enactment of the determinations of the maxim and the freedom of the will, which would be causally responsible for the enactment. So, if the determinations of the maxim are to remain temporally interrelated among themselves as constituents of the action, the causal relation between the will and the determinations, and hence, between the will and the action, must be àtemporal.

But this conclusion from 3.7. is not quite the proposition asserted by the epigram from the *Critique of Practical Reason*, since the àtemporality of the *causal relation* between the will and an action is not the àtemporality of the *action*, for the simple reason that the action is not the relation; it is rather a term of the relation, viz., its consequent. Moreover, I have argued for the àtemporality of the causal relation between the will and the enactment of the maxim in an action on the ground that the temporal relations among just the determinations of the maxim of the action would be distinct from any temporal relation between the will and the action. It may seem odd that I should be able to conclude the àtemporality of the action from the temporality of its determinations; but the oddness should disappear once it is realized that the temporality of the determinations is distinct from any such temporal relation as that which would obtain between the will and the action, and it is that distinctness from the latter temporal relation that entails that the action does not exist in a such a temporal relation as the latter one, and hence does not exist in the time that is mentioned in the epigram. Moreover, though it is true that such a temporal causal relation as that which would obtain, albeit under certain circumstances, between the will and an action would not itself *be* an action that stands in such a relation, nonetheless, the temporality of the relation between the will and the action would entail the temporality of the action, not to mention the temporality of the causality of the will, since a temporal relation between objects in general relates temporal objects. Hence, the action would be temporal. But since its own temporal nature would be incompatible with any such temporal nature of the causal relation between the will and an action, the action could not exist in such a relation with the will insofar as it consists of the determinations of its maxim that are interrelated with each other. Therefore, the conclusion of 3.7. entails the same proposition that is the conclusion of the epigram, viz., that the action in question is àtemporal. Consequently, we can conclude that 3. 7. and the epigram draw the same conclusion from apparently different premises, which, it should be said, must therefore be somehow logically related to each other.

4.2 Analysis of the Epigram

The "now" and the "long ago" of which Kant speaks in the epigram clearly belongs to the time in which there can exist what Grice and Strawson call an "ordinary" causation, as distinct from a causation in perception (see 2. above). This would be what it seems we, too, would customarily call "ordinary" or "physical" time and Kant would consider the time of empirical causal connections—the "objective succession" that he refers to in the Second Analogy of Experience. In terms of the discussion of memory in 2.6., this use of the concept of memory would conform to a use of the concept according to which the existence of the remembered object precedes the occurrence of the memory in ordinary or physical time. In that same section we discussed this possibility. For the purpose of introducing a typology of memory—a mnemonic typology—that would correspond to the typology of action that was introduced in 1.4. and employed in 2.6. n.12, the type of memory that would include the memory of an action that is described in the epigram as having occurred "long ago" would belong to Division I, Section *B* of such a mnemonic typology, a type according to which the time of the remembered object does *not* confound the memory of the object, and therefore would not be excluded from an account of the memory, since the type takes the memory to occur in ordinary or physical time, viz., only after the existence of the object as remembered in the same time.

But the point of the epigram is that it is also talking about a memory of the action insofar as the action does *not* exist in the time represented by Kant's use of "now" and "long ago"—the *ordinary* time, in which his use of the two expressions represents a *difference* in time. A memory of this type, however, since it would be a causal consequent of a causation would not conform to a *non-causal* theory of memory, since on a non-causal theory, the memory would *not* be a causal consequence of the object remembered, regardless of whether the causation would be ordinary or mnemonic. Moreover, a memory of this type does not conform to a non-causal theory of memory for another reason, viz., a non-causal theory of memory would *allow* its seeming to the agent as if she were remembering doing an action that was *other* than the one that she had in fact done "long ago" and that she "now" feels the same pangs of conscience she felt when having doing it; whereas the memory of the type in question, viz., the one the epigram pointedly implies as a memory of an action to which reason morally connects the same sensation, does *not* allow its seeming to the agent as if she were remembering doing an action that was *other* than the one that she had actually done "long ago" and that she "now" feels the same pangs of conscience she felt when having done it. In the apt expression of Strawson's (1.4.) the remembered action is a *certain* action that reason morally connects to pain, not *whatever* action happens to be given to reason for such a connection.

This leaves only Kant's *causal* theory of memory of an action to account for a memory of the type implied by the epigram—the memory besides the one that causally depends on the action in an ordinary causation in ordinary time. On Kant's causal theory of memory (following Grice's model of his causal theory of perception), the action remembered is a certain action, viz., the action pointedly implied by the epigram. But if there is not to be a logical opposition between the remembered action and the content of its memory, that is, if the memory were to be logically compatible with the remembered action, its seeming to the agent as if she were remembering the action as something she did "long ago" would be impossible. For it would not be the case that reason would always morally connect the same sensation to an action that would be such that the agent had done it "long ago." On the contrary, over time, actions are variously accompanied by pleasure and pain, depending on the circumstances and conditions under which their respective maxims are enacted, and therefore independently of any act of reason according to the moral law. Reason does not morally connect the same sensation to an action that exists in ordinary time. It rather morally connects the same sensation to an action that does *not* exist in such a time in which actions are *variously* accompanied by pleasure and pain, and not always connected by reason to the *same* sensation, which in our case would be pain.

If we now apply Kant's causal theory of memory to an action that conforms to his causal theory of action, we get the following results. Since on Kant's causal theory of memory the role of the action in the causal origin of its memory would be logically necessary for the Gricean-style mental states of the agent to constitute a memory of the action, and since on Kant's causal theory of action the role of the will in the causal origin of its action would be logically necessary for the determinations of a chosen maxim to constitute an action of the will, the memory of the action would causally depend on the will of the agent to enact the maxim of the action, assuming the transitivity of causal dependence. Since, as I argue below (5.4.), the maxim of an action determines whether the action is morally forbidden or not and its being forbidden is necessary if reason is to always morally connect pain to such an action, the causal dependence of the memory of the action on the will to enact its maxim is the causal ground on the basis of which the epigram can conclude that the memory of the action is always accompanied by pain, if it is forbidden, given the role of reason in making the connection. It is the causal dependence of the memory of the action on the will's enactment of its maxim that is the causal ground of the agent's remembering the forbidden action with the pain that reason morally connects to it—which would help causally explain the present return of the pain originally felt "long ago," viz., the pain felt "now."

5 The New Problem of the Imputability of Actions

5.1 The New Problem of the Imputability of Actions

3. above rejected interpretations of Kant's theories of action, whether causal or non-causal (as that distinction is understood in this book, which was explained in 1. and in 3.), that assumed that the *maxim* of an action is a *causal antecedent* of the will with respect to the will's *causal efficacy regarding the maxim that constitutes its action* (henceforth referred to as: CEMA). It rejected these interpretations after consideration of three alternative views of an action of the will. 3. left only one of them, viz., the view of an action from the standpoint of Kant's causal theory of action, as the theory is described in that chapter as well as in 1., as a way to view an action as an effect of the will and constituted by the *maxim* of the action. An action that results from a condition of the will that is an effect *on* the will by an external object or condition, however, is not constituted by a maxim, but, on the contrary, is a term in what Kant would consider a *natural* causation and Grice, an *ordinary* causation—an effect that is causally connected to the will by a *natural* law, instead of a *practical* law. The will would then be only a link in a historical chain of causes and effects, where antecedent causal conditions would enable or prevent the existence an action, but would have nothing to do with the maxim, or the *material* or *empirical content*, the action would have if the will were to activate a *maxim* that would determine or describe the action in the terms on which the agent acts and which the agent views as valid only for herself. Moreover, the maxim could determine or describe an action without *confounding* it, or creating a *discrepancy*, or a *mismatch*, between itself and the will, only if the will's CEMA were causally *independent* of every such external object or condition. To sum up, it was argued in 3. that since an action of the will is its effect, its maxim is a determination or description of *just* its effect, not its CEMA, since, àla Hume, the maxim cannot belong to the cause of an action without making it impossible for it to determine or describe the action, i.e. the effect, thereby leaving the action, or the effect, without any determination or description of its own apart from its cause, which would leave it completely unspecified and unknown in its own terms, a conclusion that verges on incoherence.

Correcting this fundamental reversal of what I consider the correct order between cause and effect in these misleading interpretations of Kant's theory of action, a reversal that would be destructive in a causal explanation of *any* phenomenon, as I have tried to correct for the error in 3., only creates a problem of its own, however. It is this new problem that, though it is related to one that has already appeared in the Kant literature and goes back at least to one interpretation of Kant's notion of free will that was advanced by Henry Sidgwick over a century ago, is nonetheless independent of Sidgwick's problem and therefore must survive even the best attempts to solve his particular problem.[1] Consequently, if the new problem of imputability of immoral actions to free agents can be solved, it must be done independently of any attempted solution along Sidgwickian lines. Solutions that address the problem of the imputability of forbidden actions by adopting merely Sidgwick's "Neutral" or "Moral" sense of "free will" and proceeding from there will simply leave the new problem of imputatibilty intact.

Sidgwick's problem with Kant's theory is based on the "reciprocity" Kant asserts between morality and the freedom of the will: morality, or the moral law, is possible only if the will is free, and, reciprocally, this freedom can be known only through consciousness of morality, or the moral law (G 4:446–7, KpV 5:29). It thus understandably seemed to Sidgwick that free will can act only under the idea of the moral law, or subject to moral laws, which entails that free will is incompatible with immoral action. At least such would be the entailment under *one* reading of Kant's sense of "free will" that Sidgwick finds in his reading of Kantian texts—the "Rational" or "Good" reading of the term as it appears in these texts. But Sidgwick also finds another sense of the term—the "Neutral" or the "Moral" sense of the term—that *does* accord with Kant's imputing immoral maxims, and thus the actions that they constitute, to agents whose will is free, and therefore does not present the problem presented by the first reading, though Sidgwick finds that since this other sense of "free will" has the problem of getting reconciled with the first sense, the one that engendered much of the appeal that "free will" had for Kant's readers, Kant's theory of free will would lose much of its appeal. The entailment of this more appealing sense of the term—again, the sense in which "free will" means "Rational" or "Good" will—seemed to Sidgwick to obtain, aside from his plausible reading of the many textual occurrences of the term that he cites, on the ground already briefly given just above, viz., that since causality entails a causal law between cause and effect, and the freedom of the will constitutes its causality with respect to an action, and, crucially, *the will is free only if it is "rational" or "good," and thus only under the moral law*, the will can bring about its action only under the moral law. But that seems to entail that the action is moral. Since on Kant's moral theory imputation of an action to an agent entails the agent's free will, it would then

---

[1] Henry Sidgwick, "Appendix, The Kantian Conception of Free Will," in *The Methods of Ethics*, seventh edition, (Indianapolis, IN: Hackett Publishing Company, Inc., 1981, first published 1907), pp. 511–16.

be impossible to impute an *immoral* action to the agent—the quite unwelcome conclusion Sidgwick took from one of his readings of Kant's two senses of the term. It is especially unwelcome once it is realized that if only moral actions can be imputed to a free agent, *no* action at all can be imputed to an agent, since the morality of an action would be indistinguishable from its imputability and would therefore be otiose. Moral ascription would then collapse into causal attribution, thereby preventing the nomenclature of "morality" from adding anything significant to an action or to the will that had not already been considered to be *causally* responsible for the action. Causality would simply verbally masquerade as morality (which unfortunately it sometimes does, in the mouths of bombasts). Sidgwick thus set the stage for subsequent scholarship on Kant's problem of the imputability of immoral or forbidden actions to free agents.

But, as already indicated, even if Sidgwick's wider "Neutral" or "Moral" sense of "freedom" allows the term to be applied to forbidden actions of a free agent without contradicting the sense of "morality," the sense that accords much better with Kant's moral theory than the narrower sense of "free will" (as "Rational" or "Good"), there remains the independent problem of this very causal attribution of forbidden actions to free agents who act in accordance with the moral law, a problem that, being independent of the ambiguity that Sidgwick finds in Kant's uses of "free will," is not only not obviated by simply opting for the "Neutral" or "Moral" sense of "freedom" and thereby removing the ambiguity presented by the other sense of "freedom," but is openly displayed without the obscurity created by the other sense of the term hovering in its penumbra: how can a causal law be violated by its very effect, given a cause that acts in accordance with the law? Opting for the "Neutral" or "Moral" sense of "free will" only reveals the problem more vividly than before, when the problem was obscured by the ambiguity between the two senses of "free will." As I have already stated, the independent problem is actually created by the very method I myself have adopted in my rejection of the interpretations of Allison *et al.* of Kant's theory of the will's CEMA in 3. Hence, it is incumbent on me to try to solve the new, independent problem of the imputatibility of immoral actions to free agents. Any solution I might propose, however, would run the risk of being unintelligible unless the grounds for the problem I am addressing were further clarified.

The problem arises from the shift in our interests from *justifying* the will and its action in terms of practical *normative* law to *causally connecting* the will and its action in terms of the same law, only, now, it is *causal* law. As remarked in our discussion of Quine in 1., he, too, shifts the attention of epistemology away from *justification* of theoretical expressions in terms of sensory vocabulary to genetic, even causal, explanation of the empirical meaning of the sensory terms themselves, an explanation in terms of stimulations of the senses. But our Kantian shift to causal explanation of action requires the distinction between natural causal explanation of an event in terms of the causal efficacy of another event and practical causal explanation of an action in terms of a will that is independent of every external object and condition. The distinction entails the further distinction between a natural causal law that *cannot* allow an effect to violate the law and the practical causal law that *can* allow the law to be violated by the effect. In the very beginning of the *Critique of Practical Reason*, Kant makes this latter distinction the central difference between the two kinds of causal law—free, or practical, and natural (KpV 5:19–20). It is the difference that precisely corresponds to the difference that Sidgwick found in Kant's two senses of "free will": the *impossibility* of the violation of the causal law that attaches to both natural law and to practical law according to the "Rational" or "Good" sense of "free will," and the *possibility* of the same violation in the "Neutral" or "Moral" sense of the same term, "free will." But I am drawing attention to the fact that attaching the latter sense to "free will" is not a solution to the *new* problem of the imputability of immoral or forbidden actions to free agents, though it does solve the problem of ambiguity between two senses of Kant's "free will" and thereby solves the problem of the imputability of immoral actions to agents whose free will is understood in the "Neutral" or "Moral" sense of "free will." Attaching the latter sense to "free will" only reveals the new problem of imputatibility clearly for all to see: *how can the will can bring about an action that violates the very causal law that makes its existence possible (by causally connecting it to the will)*? Whereas the old Sidgwickian problem of imputability stemmed from a forbidden action's violation of the practical *normative* law, which Sidgwick identifies with the "Neutral" or "Moral" sense of "free will," the new problem consists in accepting that identification and then asking about the possibility of an action's violation of the practical *causal* law—the *causal* connection between free will and the action, which is actually closer to Sidgwick's "Rational" or "Good" sense of "free will."

In order to see how the new problem of imputatibility arises directly from my adoption of the third of the alternative views of an action in 3., it should be recalled that one conclusion of that chapter was that the will's CEMA is causally independent of every external object or condition (as is Sidgwick's "Rational" or "Good" sense of "free will"). The will's CEMA therefore clearly places the maxim of an action on the side of the *effect*, i.e. the action, with respect to the terms of the causal relation between the will's CEMA and an action, whereas the interpretations that were rejected place the maxim of an action among the causal *antecedents* of the will's CEMA. Now, however, it is precisely the *correct* placement of the maxim of an action in the causal relation between the will and an action that gives rise to the new problem. The problem now is, how the moral law can *causally* connect the will to an effect that violates the very law on which the existence of the effect obviously causally depends, something that is incomprehensible with respect to natural causal law. Whereas the old problem was the apparent impossibility of reconciling an act of free will under the moral law with the will's bringing about an immoral action, an impossibility that stemmed specifically from Kant's use of the "Rational" or "Good" sense of "free will" when the possibility of an immoral action required the "Neutral" or "Moral" sense of "free will," thereby creating the impossibility of any reconciliation between the free will and the forbidden actions, since the two senses of "free will" were mutually contrary, the new problem of imputing an immoral action to a free will is that if an immoral maxim does not belong to a free will's CEMA but belongs instead to the *effect* of the CEMA, as I have argued that it must, the general problem of imputability returns, only now it is the more specific question of how the law constituting the causal connection between the will and an action whose immorality is constituted by its maxim can violate the very law that helps make the existence of the violation, i.e. the existence of the action, possible. It defies our conception of causal law, if that conception is based on natural causal law. The new problem is not which sense of "free will" to adopt, but whichever sense is adopted, how can a law connect a cause and an effect, if the effect does not conform to the law?

5.2 The Moral Law is the Practical Causal Law

What, then, is the relation between the practical causal law that connects the will and a forbidden action, on the one hand, and the moral law, or the Categorical Imperative, which forbids the action, on the other hand? Are they the same law? That is a question I raised in the second section of the Preface to the book and is the *first* question I want to raise in this section of this chapter, and the answer I proposed in the Preface is that for Kant they are indeed the same law: the moral law *is* the causal law that connects the will and an action. Accordingly, it is the *practical causal law* that Kant also calls *the moral law*.

I cannot state my grounds for the proposal more succinctly than I have in the Preface. To reiterate, Kant himself makes the identification in Section III of the *Groundwork* (G 4:446–7, 4:457, 4:460), among other places, including the Third Antinomy in the *Critique of Pure Reason*. Second, a basis for his making the identification is his conception of causal law according to which an "effect can be posited" if something is thought or called a "cause" (G 4:446–7). Effects, then, can be posited according to causal laws as consequents of such conditional propositions, provided that objects thought or called "cause" occur as antecedents. If this conception of causal law is applied to the relation between the will and an action, it is from the practical causal law that an action of the will can be posited as the consequent of the law, provided the will is thought or called the "cause" of the action. A third and final, but related, reason for Kant's identification of the practical causal law as the moral law is that if the causal law connecting the will and an action were a *natural* law, it would be plain nonsense to consider the action *forbidden* (KrV A 547/B575). Together, these considerations lead to the conclusion that the practical causal law is the moral law, if a theory of forbidden actions as effects of the will is to be possible.

5.3 Solutions to the Old Imputability Problem

It may seem that the new imputability problem has already been addressed, perhaps inadvertently, by others whose ostensible concern was the old imputability problem, and here I am referring specifically to the Anglophone literature on Kant's moral theory. I would not of course be proposing my own solution to the new problem on Kant's behalf if I had found any of their solutions to the old problem adequate to solve the new one. I will consider just three solutions that have been put forward by scholars still active in Kant's moral theory and that seem to me to fail to deal with the new problem. The first solution—to the old problem, to be sure—has been proposed by Allen Wood. He claims that the *causal* connection for Kant between the will and an action is a *normative* relation, in the sense that it is a "principle according to which [the will] *ought* to act," and thus is "an imperative."[2] He describes cases of actions that "*contravene*" norms as "*failed attempts* to comply with the norm."[3] In clear coordination with his agreement with Allison that the maxim of an action is to be considered an antecedent causal condition of the causal relation between the will and an action and thus placed on the side of the will's CEMA, Wood also places the norms that guide the will in its taking an action on the side of the will's CEMA, instead of on the side of the will's effect, i.e. the action taken. Since the new problem of imputability is that forbidden actions are *successful attempts* of the will to produce an action according to a practical causal law and the new problem is to explain that possibility, Wood's interpretation of Kant that norms that are violated by actions are part of "*failed attempts* to comply with the

---

[2] Allen W. Wood, *Kant's Ethical Thought* (Cambridge, UK: Cambridge University Press, 1999), p. 172.
[3] Wood, *Kant's Ethical Thought*, p. 173.

norm[s]" simply does not deal with the new problem. His notion of "*Freedom through causality of norms,*" where the causal role of the moral law *includes* its normative role, can have nothing to do with the new problem, since the success of the freedom of the will through the causality of norms that help produce forbidden actions has nothing to do with any (for Kant clearly spurious) *causal* origin of, specifically, the *immorality* of the actions and not merely the *existence* of the actions, since it would make no sense to *causally* attribute the *immorality* of actions to the *norms* that played a role in the (causal) origin of the mere *existence* of the actions, although the norms obviously played a non-causal but nonetheless *normative* role in the ascription of their immorality. Considerations such as these that are made here against Wood's interpretation are similar to Sidgwick's distinction of Kant's sense of "free will" as "Rational" or "Good" from its sense as "Neutral" or "Moral." For the same reason, Wood's inclusion of an agent's *intentions* as normative causal laws also bypasses the new problem of imputability. Wood says "people can bungle intended actions or fail to carry through their intentions."[4] But, again, the new problem concerns forbidden actions that are actually *produced* by the will, not failures of the will; it concerns the *existence* of *immoral* actions, not the *non-existence* of *moral* ones. Finally, Wood restricts intentions to "pursue an end" to Kant's hypothetical imperatives.[5] But hypothetical imperatives fail to be practical *laws* for Kant, since the necessity of a law for him is *unconditional*, in the sense that it is the necessity of a rule that does not vary from person to person or vary at different times in a person's lifetime, whereas the necessity of a hypothetical imperative *is* conditional in that very sense; that is, hypothetical imperatives determine actions that are means to *ends* that *do* vary from person to person and vary even for the same person during her lifetime. To sum up our albeit brief examination Wood's interpretation of Kant's account of forbidden actions, it simply does not deal with the problem of forbidden actions that is of concern to us, viz., forbidden actions that the will *succeeds* in bringing about according to the very practical causal law that the actions violate, viz., the moral law.

Henry Allison's interpretation of Kant's account of the causality of the freedom of the will has the same problem as Wood's interpretation regarding forbidden actions. According to Allison's interpretation, since a causal law is "normally" thought to assert a "necessary connection between causes and effects"—a conception that treats the law as what Allison calls a "*modus operandi* "—the moral law fits that conception of causal law only if the moral law is applied to a "hypothetical perfectly

---

4 Wood, *Kant's Ethical Thought*, p. 173.
5 Wood, *Kant's Ethical Thought*, p. 173.

rational agent."[6] Since human beings are "imperfectly rational beings," the moral law cannot be thought to assert a "necessary connection between causes and effects."[7] The moral law for human beings connects the will to an action, not in the relation of causes and effects, but, and here Allison's position is just like Wood's, in the relation of *obligation*—a *"modus obligandi,"* as Allison calls it, thereby indicating a *distinction* between an *imperative* and a *causal* connection.[8] Since the problem of forbidden actions caused by the will according to the moral law takes the connection to be causal in precisely the way that Allison says it is not causal, Allison too, like Wood, only bypasses the problem of the will's causing forbidden actions according to the practical causal law.

There is another problem with Allison's solution besides its bypassing the new imputability problem. Allison attributes to his "Incorporation Thesis" (discussed in 3.) that maxims must spontaneously, i.e. freely, incorporate incentives, including those from inclination, if the incentives are to play a role in the causal origin of an action, the causal efficacy regarding action that non-Kantians, especially those adopting the Humean desire-belief "model," attribute instead to bare inclination in a naturalistic or deterministic causal explanation of action. With respect to the "act of incorporation," Allison says that "it is the genuine causal factor" in Kant's theory of freedom.[9] Allison is quite aware, however, that Kant holds that something's efficacy with respect to an effect entails a causal law according to which the effect occurs. Moreover, he is also explicit that the only law recognized by Kant that could do the job that causally connects Kant's will and an action is the moral law, since the only other law recognized by Kant, natural law, would reduce moral explanation to natural explanation, thereby undoing ethics altogether for Kant. Unfortunately for the consistency of Allison's interpretation of Kant's theory of freedom, however, we have just seen that Allison explicitly denies that Kant's moral law can be correctly interpreted as a relation between cause and effect; it must rather, he says, be understood as a relation of obligation. But that leaves the causal efficacy of the Incorporation Thesis without a causal law, since now the moral law has been reformulated as a law of obligation, not a causal connection, and natural law is unfit for employment in moral theory. Without a causal law, however, since causality entails law, Allison ought to withdraw the causal efficacy he earlier in his work attributes to the Incorporation Thesis. The unwelcome result for his theory of freedom is that it provides no consistent account whatsoever of freedom's causal connection to action.

---

6 Allison, *Kant's Theory of Freedom* (Cambridge, UK: Cambridge University Press, 1990), p. 244.
7 Allison, *Kant's Theory of Freedom*, p. 214
8 Allison, *Kant's Theory of Freedom*, p. 214
9 Allison, *Kant's Theory of Freedom*, p. 51.

5.3 Solutions to the Old Imputability Problem — 69

Christine Korsgaard offers a radical solution to the old problem of imputability. Rather than trying to reconcile forbidden actions with free will and the moral law she finds them incompatible. Forbidden actions are indeed not imputable to the free will that produces them according to the moral law. But that is not a problem, since the very attempt at imputation is a mistake. There are, following Kant's own use of the idea (e.g., G 4:452), two "standpoints" one can take with respect to forbidden actions, she claims on her interpretation of Kant's theory of freedom and its relation to forbidden actions.[10] One is the practical standpoint, which presupposes the will is free, or spontaneous, and acts under the moral law. The other standpoint is theoretical, which does not make that presupposition, but rather takes the agent to produce a forbidden action in a deterministic system under natural law, perhaps in the expectation of gratifying an inclination of hers. To ask, therefore, how by means of her free will under the moral law she can commit a forbidden action is to incoherently place her simultaneously at both standpoints. Her freely taking an action under the moral law is intelligible only from the practical standpoint, but her committing a forbidden action according to a determination of inclination is intelligible only from the theoretical standpoint. In committing a forbidden action, the agent forsakes the freedom of her will under the moral law for the expected gratification of her inclination. To ask of the free will under the determination of the moral law how it could be responsible for forbidden actions is therefore to ask for the impossible. Korsgaard's solution to the old problem of imputability thus amounts to a rejection of the very significance of the old problem as well as, it should be added, the significance of the new problem. Since Wood, Allison, and we ourselves are trying to understand the possibility of free forbidden actions, Korsgaard is telling us that the very attempt to understand that possibility reveals a failure to keep the two standpoints distinct, since the freedom of forbidden actions places the agent at the very standpoint that the agent has abandoned—the practical one. The agent has done so, Korsgaard claims, for the sake of pursuing the object of her inclination, which puts her squarely into the deterministic system of natural law.[11] Only incoherence can result from this conflation of the agent's position at each standpoint. With respect to the application of Korsgaard's approach to the new problem of imputability, however, she does share with Wood and Allison the feature of bypassing the new problem, viz., again, how the result of the will producing an action according to the moral law can be a violation of the law. Where Wood answered, that though the causal relation between the will and the action is a nor-

---

10 Christine Korsgaard, *Creating the Kingdom of Ends* (Cambridge, UK: Cambridge University Press, 1996), pp. 173 ff.
11 Korsgaard, *Creating the Kingdom of Ends*, pp. 173 ff.

mative relation, in the case of a forbidden action the will does not actually *succeed* in producing the requisite or intended action, and where Allison answered, that the relation between the will and the action according to the moral law is not really a causal relation at all, but is instead a normative or obligatory one, Korsgaard responds that the very question we are raising is incoherent, since it fails to see that by just *asking* the question we are placing the agent at two incompatible standpoints simultaneously, the practical and the theoretical, and asking how, by means of the agent's will, the agent can freely do according to the moral law what can only be done deterministically according to a natural law. So, once again, now grouped with Wood, Allison, Korsgaard bypasses the new imputability problem in favor of her preferred solution to the old one.

5.4 The Solution to the New Imputability Problem

The solution to the new imputability problem can be found, I propose, not in the connection itself—not in the law—but in the only other possible place it might be found, viz., in the subject whose will is the cause of the action. This would entail that the subject contains the grounds for the violation of the law and that these grounds would of course be logically independent of the law, and conversely, the law would be logically independent of the grounds. But since they would be grounds for an action's being forbidden by the very law that connects the will to the action, and hence would be grounds for a violation that leaves the causal connection *intact*, that is, the forbidden action would still be the result of the will according to the causal law, there must be a *relation* between the grounds for the violation and the causal law itself.

What Kant calls the *maxim* of an action alone can contain the grounds of forbidden action we are looking for. As a fundamental practical proposition that is regarded by the subject as valid for herself alone the maxim of an action in general is logically independent of the law, which is known purely *a priori* and so holds for every possible subject, and conversely (KpV 5:19). In other words, since a maxim in general is regarded by each subject as valid only for herself, so regarded, it is different for each one. But, necessarily, it is precisely the *differences* among subjects that are logically independent of the law known purely *a priori* that holds for all of them, and conversely, necessarily, the law is logically independent of the differences among the subjects.

Since the will for Kant is the source of practical causal law and the law cannot account for the specifically forbidden quality of the actions that result according to the law, which leaves it to the maxims of the actions to account for their being forbidden, Kant's theory of forbidden action requires a means other than the will by which the subject can form and adopt a *fundamental practical proposition* (KpV 5:19) that can be her maxim of a forbidden action, as well as proposition that can be her maxim of a *permissible* action. Kant identifies the means in question as the power of free choice (*Willkür*), a faculty to which he assigns, in the first and the second *Critiques* and in *The Metaphysics of Morals*, the subject's free choice of the proposition or principle according to which she acts, and thus the maxim of her action.

Next, we must address the relation between a maxim and the practical causal law that is necessary if an action is to result from the will. Though an action can result from the will only according to the law, we have just seen that requirement to be only a *necessary* condition of the possibility that a determination of the will is a determination of an action; we have seen that the possibility of an action also requires the involvement of the maxim of the action. Accordingly, a determination of the will can be a determination of an action according to practical causal law iff a determination is also contained in the maxim of the action, where the latter determination is not necessarily the former one nor is it necessary that the latter determination *conforms* to the former determination.

This statement of the relation between a maxim and the practical law applies to the same relation that is involved in the possibility of a *forbidden* action. In such a case the relation must be *conflict* (KpV 5:19, *et passim*)—the precise relation that is missing from any putative *natural* causal connection between the will and an action, and more generally, missing from any natural causal connection between any cause and any effect. Without a conflict between the maxim of an action and the practical causal law that connects the will to a forbidden action, we cannot understand the result of the will according to the law to be forbidden. Kant's solution, I propose, is that *an action results from the will according to the practical causal law—the moral law; but the action is forbidden because its maxim conflicts with the law*. An action is both a *result* of the will according to the practical causal law and an *object* of the subject's *maxim*, that is, an object of the proposition (*Satz*) or principle (*Prinzip*) according to which the subject acts, and the maxim may conflict with the law, which it does just in case the action is forbidden. So, an action is *both* an *effect* according to one type of fundamental practical proposition for Kant –the practical causal law—and an *object* of a different type of fundamental practical proposition for him—the maxim of an action. It is due to this two-fold nature of an action that it can be *both* a *result* of the will according to the practical causal *law and* an *object* of an immoral *maxim*, and thus can be a *forbidden action*. *If we can combine these two sides of an action we can conclude that the will can produce an object of an immoral maxim—a forbidden action—only according to the moral law.*

5.5 Laws of Freedom and Laws of Nature and the Solution to the New Problem of Imputability

The contrast between a causal law of freedom and a natural causal law can account for the following solution to the new problem of imputability as well as a solution to the old problem. If it is the freedom of the will that is involved in the causal law of freedom, free will produces an action internally. Without dependence on a prior cause, there is no law that connects the will to an external cause of the will. Consequently, the law that connects the will to its effect is also internal to the will. However, as already noted, the will and the law cannot account for the *differences* among the determinations of an effect or among the determinations of many effects, and hence the will plus the law cannot account for the determinations that distinguish the various elements of an action from one another or that distinguish various actions from one another. These would be determinations that are external to the will and the law and would be determinations of *just the effect(s)*. Consequently, the will plus the law cannot account for the determinations of *just the effect(s)*; the account must rather be external to the will and the law, even though the will produces the effect(s) *only according to the law*. Only the maxim of the action can account for the determinations of just the effect(s), i.e. of just the action(s), which implies the need for the maxim(s) of the action(s). One such determination might result in an action's being forbidden, another in an action's being permissible.

The situation is reversed regarding natural causal law. There, determinations that are prior and external to the cause determine *just the cause* in their role as "given conditions." Consequently, a law connecting the cause and the effect would be external to the cause, since the law would need to connect these external determinations with the cause. Together, these external determinations of *just the cause* plus the law *would* be sufficient to account for the determinations of the effect: no further determinations external to the cause besides those on which its causality already depends would be necessary to posit determinations of the effect according to the law. For example, increasing the pressure on some completely enclosed volume of gas results in increased temperature of the gas according to the gas law. The increase in pressure on the gas is external to the gas as is the law that connects the increase in pressure to the gas; if the law were not external to, or independent of, the gas, it could not explain how an increase in pressure results in an increase in temperature. The increase in pressure on the gas is among the "given conditions" that produce, or explain, the increase in temperature according to the gas law. There are no determinations of the increase in temperature that are independent of the given conditions and the gas law: the given conditions plus the law are sufficient to imply the increase in temperature. The increase in the temperature of the gas is thus *determined* by the given conditions according to the law.

A causal law of freedom and a causal law of nature can therefore be distinguished if *determinations that are external to the cause of an effect* are divided between determinations of *just the effect* and determinations of *just the cause*. *Determinations that are external to the cause of an effect are determinations of just the effect iff the causal law is a law of freedom,* and *determinations that are external to the cause of an effect are determinations of just the cause iff the causal law is a law of nature.*

If we call determinations that are external to the cause "*front-loaded*" iff they are determinations of *just the cause* and "*end-loaded*" iff they are determinations of *just the effect*, then a causal connection according to a law of freedom would be *end-loaded* and a causal connection according to a natural law would be *front-loaded*. Accordingly, a law of freedom that connects a cause and an effect would leave the effect *undetermined*, since the cause and the law cannot account for the determinations of just the effect that are external to the cause and that are therefore *end-loaded:* the cause plus the law cannot possibly account for these determinations of the effect. This would suggest an understanding of the *freedom* of the cause's efficacy as the freedom of *indeterminism* and an understanding of the *determinism* of a cause's efficacy as the *determinism* of nature iff the law is natural. But the suggestion cannot be left there, since it would leave out the *end-loaded* determinations of a causation of freedom. An interpretation of Kant's notion of freedom, especially, the freedom of the will, as *indeterminism*—a doctrine that would keep the will from enjoying the power of causality because of the absence of a causal law that could connect the will to a *determined* effect—would be an interpretation that fails to take into account the end-loaded nature of a causation that occurs according to a law of freedom. Though the cause and a law of freedom cannot determine the effect, it does not follow that the effect is *indeterminate*, though it is *undetermined* by the cause plus the law. Hence, it does not follow that the freedom of the cause is to be understood as *indeterminism*, although that is suggested by the statement that the effect is undetermined by the cause plus the law. Rather, we can say that while the effect is determinate, its determinations that are external to its cause are *end-loaded*; that is, not only are they external to the cause, but they are determinations of *just the effect*. Consequently, freedom is not indeterminism; it is rather a causality that is limited with respect to the determinations of its effect. A cause that produces its effect according to a law of freedom cannot determine its effect with respect to determinations that are *end-loaded, since these determinations of effects belong to their subjective uptake*—the taking up of the determinations into either the empirical *intuition* of an *appearance*, if the cause (of the appearance) is noumenal, or a thing in itself, or the empirical *maxim* of an *action*, if the cause (of the action) is the freedom of the will. Those determinations, being taken up into, and therefore belonging to, (subjective) empirical intuitions or (subjective) maxims, are, *in that specific respect of being taken up*, independent of the (objective) cause of the appearance or the action.[12]

Determinations that are *external* to the cause of an effect in the specified respect in which they are *independent* of the cause are unavoidable, that is, the respect in which the determinations are taken up into empirical intuitions of appearances or maxims of actions; theory must therefore deal with them insofar as they are considered in that specified respect. The only question for theory is, how are they loaded, front- or end-loaded; alternatively, is the effect undetermined or determined by the cause plus the law? In an age such as ours—contemporary philosophy in the empiricist tradition of analytic philosophy—we naturally take external determinations in the specified respect to be *front-loaded*, and thus effects to be *determined*. But in early modern philosophy in the rationalist tradition of systematic philosophy, they naturally took external determinations in the specified respect to be *end-loaded*, and thus effects to be *undetermined*. Both schools of philosophy still have to deal with their counterpart's preference: empiricism must deal rationalism's end-loading and rationalism with empiricism's front-loading. One may pronounce the other's rule that relates antecedent and consequent not a genuine causal law. But it does seem to "level the playing field," to speak in a more neutral and non-partisan language, and thus remove the prejudgment against rationalism in today's age of empiricist philosophy in the Anglophone tradition, if we were to view the dispute about causal law and determined or undetermined effects as the question of whether determinations that are external to the cause of an effect in the specified respect are to be end-loaded or front-loaded, given that the determinations are unavoidable in any case and exist regardless of whether the philosopher's predilections are empiricist or rationalist.

5.6 Hud Hudson's Front-loading

A case in point would be a certain dispute among philosophers over Kant's theory of freedom. I for one will employ the notion of *end-loaded causations* to respond to an interpretation of Kant's theory of freedom as a form of *indeterminism*

---

12 Such a limitation by the subjective conditions of the recipient of an action creates a need for a "*critique*" of pure reason, whether pure reason is theoretical, that is, transcendental, or practical.

advanced by Hud Hudson.[13] Hudson's explicit concern here is not the problem of the imputability of forbidden actions to the agent, though that problem, old or new, is involved,[14] but the issue of a compatibilism between Kant's theory of freedom and his theory of the determinism of nature. Hudson position is that Kant is a compatibilist. If he can show that Kant's freedom of the will is compatible with the determinism of nature, he will have made his point. The key to his argument is that he interprets Kant's notion of the freedom of the will as a form of indeterminism.[15] He successfully argues that the will plus the moral law leaves the action *undetermined*. He then draws his conclusion concerning indeterminism and hence compatibilism. Since indeterminism for Hudson is the insufficiency of an antecedent plus a rule to entail a consequent *all the relations among whose necessary properties are determined by a causal law*, thereby making the consequent a *determined* object in the sense italicized, and since he insists on such sufficiency for a rule to count as a causal law, Hudson follows Ralf Meerbote[16] who, in turn, relies on Donald Davidson's theory of anomalous monism—the theory that mental representations are ungoverned by law—to look outside the mind to get a causal law, which would therefore connect the will to a *determined* action, again, *determined* in the sense italicized just above.[17] Assuming, following Davidson again, a token-token identity between mental and physical states, Hudson finds natural or physical law as the causal connection between the will and the determinations of an action that is thereby determined, in the italicized sense, by the physical correspondence of the will and the physical causal law. Freedom and the moral law thus play no role in the causal origin of a *determined* action, in the sense italicized, apart from the token-token identity and the physical causal law.

Not only does Hudson's theory run counter to the proposition on which our interpretation of Kant is based, viz., that the practical causal law is the moral law, but it does not take into account the possibility of understanding Kant's theory of a law of freedom as it has been explained here. Freedom of the will would be indeterminism as Hudson alleges were it not for *end-loaded* causations, which are free—causations that admittedly leave an action *undetermined*,

---

[13] Hud Hudson, *Kant's Compatibilism* (Ithaca, NY and London: Cornell University Press, 1994).
[14] Hudson, *Kant's Compatibilism*, pp. 149 ff.
[15] Hudson, *Kant's Compatibilism*, pp. 53–5.
[16] Ralf Meerbote, "Kant on the Nondeterminate Character of Human Actions," in *Kant on Causality, Freedom, and Objectivity*. ed. William Harper and Ralf Meerbote (Minneapolis: University of Minnesota Press, 1984), p. 139.
[17] Donald Davidson, "Mental Events," in *Essays on Actions and Events* (Oxford, UK: Oxford Clarendon Press, 1980), pp. 208–11.

in the italicized sense of *determined:* only the effects of *front-loaded* causations are *determined* in the italicized sense. So, the causal law remains the moral law, but since it is a law of freedom, the determinations of just the action must nonetheless be *external to*, or *independent of*, the will, *in the respect specified* above, and thus must be *end-loaded* onto free causations, even though the action is still produced by the will according to the law. Hence, although the action is not left indeterminate—its maxim's making it determinate—the law of freedom becomes a form of indeterminism on Hudson's notion of indeterminism, since the action is still *undetermined* by the will according to a causal law of freedom, in the italicized sense of *determined*.

This indeterminism keeps a law of freedom from being a causal law only on the assumption that only laws of determinism, i.e. natural laws, that is, causal connections that are *front-loaded*, are causal laws. And that is obviously not Kant's assumption. For Kant, practical causal law does not entail that the action is determined, in the italicized sense, precisely because causal laws of freedom do not have that entailment and practical causal law is a causal law of freedom. Rather, the determinations of an action, in the specified respect, are taken up into empirical intuitions of appearances or maxims of actions from sources that reside in the subject's sensibility (intuitions) or incentives (maxims). Though these determinations of actions, which are considered as belonging to maxims, are not the result of any causal law, practical or natural, that does not disqualify them from being determinations of their respective actions. Being a direct result of a causal law is not a logically necessary condition of a determination of an action; a maxim is not itself the direct result of practical causal law even if contains the incentive that consists of respect for moral duty, an incentive that *would* be a direct result of practical causal law, since the subject must take up the incentive into the maxim of an action for it to be a determination of an action, in the respect that has been specified. The necessary uptake is a logical consequence of the fact that the maxim is an instance of the concept of a maxim, or a maxim in general, and a maxim in general cannot be a direct result of the law, since that would rule out maxims whose incentives originate externally to the law and thus to the will to which it is internal. Finally, Hudson's recourse to Davidson's reliance on physical, and thus natural, law to account for the determinations of actions actually makes things worse for Kant, at least on the usual reading of Kant. For the effect of the will according to natural law on our account of Kant's theory actually *front-loads* the causation with given conditions. The only law that could connect the conditions or prior cause with the will would be a law that would be external to the will, and it would be this external law that would have to causally connect the will with an action, which is precisely what Hudson says it would have to be and would have to do. But this would leave Kant not only without a causal theory of action that distinguishes practical from theoretical philosophy, but, more to the point of our present interest, without a possible solution to the problem of imputability. To make up for this lack, and again following Meerbote,[18] Hudson proposes a solution that he recognizes is contradicted by what Kant actually says about practical law, viz., he proposes a practical causal law that is empirical, and thus would be a law of "empirical practical reason."[19]

5.7 The Problem of the Imputability of Actions as a Fundamental Mistake

The new problem of imputability is therefore based on a mistake, as is the old problem: to ask how actions can be forbidden, given the will and the moral law, is to ask a question that can be asked of a law only if it is a natural law—a law external to the will—and of a will whose power to cause its effect is subject to determinations that are external to it. Since the determination of being forbidden is a determination that is *both* external to the will, and thus to the moral law, *and* is a determination of *just the action* and not of the will and therefore not of the moral law, only the *maxim* of the action can answer the question. Asked of the will and a *natural* law, the question cannot even arise, for then although the given determinations of the will and a natural law would, *per impossible*, be sufficient to account for forbidden actions, the actions could not be *forbidden!*

Consequently, forbidden actions can still be as successfully imputed to the will according to the moral law as they were at the start of our discussion; free will would still be responsible for forbidden actions, since it would still produce the object of an immoral maxim according to the moral law and the immorality of a maxim would still depend on whether or not the maxim conflicts with the law. The will and the law together just could not determine the actual presence or absence of such a conflict and therefore could not determine an action's actually being *forbidden*, or its actually being *permissible*. Those determinations would be not only external to the will and to the moral law but also would be determinations of *just the actions* and not determinations of their cause or the law, despite the fact that it would be the law that would be the criterion of the actual morality of the actions. A determination of whether the criterion is satisfied would be a separate matter and would depend on the maxims of the actions.

---

18 Meerbote, "*Wille* and *Willkür* in Kant's Theory of Action," in *Interpreting Kant*, ed. Moltke S. Gram (Iowa City: University of Iowa Press, 1982), pp. 69–84, cited by Hudson in *Kant's Compatibilism*.
19 Hudson, *Kant's Compatibilism*, p. 159.

5.8 Korsgaard's and My Respective Corrections of the Mistake

Finally, the points of agreement between my solution to the new imputability problem and Korsgaard's solution to the old one must be acknowledged. She and I both consider the problem in general a mistake in the way of looking at the relation between the will and the moral law, on the one hand, and forbidden actions, on the other hand. Moreover, we agree that the mistake in the way of looking involves asking, as Korsgaard would say, from the practical standpoint something that can be asked intelligibly only from the theoretical standpoint, viz., in Korsgaard's formulation, how the free will under the moral law can do anything wrong (whereas I would ask how the free will can do anything wrong according to the practical causal law). Our points of agreement concern the distinct roles of the moral law and natural law in practical and theoretical philosophy, respectively, and the use of the distinction in our respective solutions to the at least *ostensibly* intelligible statements of the problem of imputability in general. We thus would agree that the problem of imputability in general rests on a mistake, and the mistake involves a confusion between what can be asked of or expected from a law of freedom, and thus, for our discussion, the moral law, or the practical causal law, and what can be asked of or expected from a natural law. We would further agree that the will and the moral, or practical causal, law together cannot answer the question of imputability intelligibly, whether the question is expressed her way or, and here I make a presumption about Korsgaard's imagined response, my way, and regardless of whether the question is asked in its old form or, again the same presumption, in its new form.

But we also have our disagreements. Where Korsgaard would regard our version of the problem as unintelligible, I obviously regard it as quite intelligible. Where she would say that the agent under moral law *cannot* freely take forbidden actions, I would say that the agent *can* freely take the actions according to the same law. Moreover, I do not agree that correcting the mistake inherent in the problem in general comes at the price of shifting the agent from the practical standpoint to the theoretical one. There is no forsaking freedom for the gratification of desire on my solution. On the contrary, the freedom of the will in producing an action according to the moral law is really as central and as intelligible on my solution to the problem as it seems to be intuitively from the standpoint of the imputation of a forbidden action to the agent. I keep the freedom of the will and the moral law in place, but rely on the maxim of an action and its possible conflict with the moral law to explain the possibility of forbidden actions. Finally, I contrast the moral law with natural law and what Kant calls the theoretical use of reason only to guard against asking of or expecting from freedom and the moral law only what determinism and natural law can provide, rather than to take the radical position of Korsgaard's that free will and the moral law are not causally involved in the existence of forbidden actions at all.

5.9 Conclusion

Though the distinction between theoretical and practical knowledge for Kant is sharp and inviolate, the relation between the subject that produces an action of a maxim by means of the (practical) freedom of its will according to practical causal law can, as I have already intermittently done above, be patterned on the causal law of transcendental freedom that connects an object of reason (a thing in itself) and the undetermined object of an empirical intuition (an appearance). Thus, the free will of the subject in Kant's theory of practical knowledge corresponds to the thing in itself in his transcendental theory of theoretical knowledge, the maxim corresponds to the empirical intuition, an object of the maxim—the action—corresponds to the object of the empirical intuition—the appearance—and the causal law of practical freedom—the moral law—corresponds to the causal law of transcendental freedom. The analogy breaks down, however, at precisely the point at which a maxim can conflict with practical causal law, since an empirical intuition cannot conflict with the theoretical causal law of transcendental freedom, and thus an appearance cannot be prohibited by the very law according to which it is produced and therefore exists.

The breakdown in the analogy is partly due to the fact that a human intuition that can agree with a causal law is a singular representation (of an object) whose form is time; but time is a form of a causal law that is *natural*—precisely the type of causal law that is *distinct* from the type involved in the analogy, i.e. a law of freedom.[20] Consequently, there cannot be an agreement of a human intuition with a causal law of *transcendental* freedom; hence, there cannot be a *conflict* between them, either. But we have seen that there can be an agreement or a conflict between a maxim and a causal law of practical freedom. Though the maxim, like the intuition, is a singular representation (i.e. a singular proposition) having reference to just the agent, it contains a *general* determination of the will—the way in which the agent acts—whereas an intuition either contains sensations—subjective mental states—in case the intuition is empirical, or it consists of *a priori* intuitive representations of the intuition's form: specifically, given our purposes in this discussion, time. The *form* of a maxim, on the other hand—the form of this practical

---

20 See 8.5. below for an argument in support of this claim.

singular proposition, which would be the counterpart to the corresponding form of an intuition, time—determines whether the maxim agrees or conflicts with the causal law of practical freedom. Since the agreement would be an agreement with the law, the form of agreement could only be the practically *legislative* form of the maxim, and the corresponding conflict could only be the absence of that form. In the second *Critique* the form of a maxim is said to depend on the *relation* between the (material) *object* of the will and the moral *law* that determines duty. The form of a maxim is *legislative*, Kant states, that is, the form of a maxim is the form of the moral law iff the relation between the maxim and the law is that the law, and therefore duty, is *prior* to the material object of the will, so that the law, and not the material object of the will, determines the maxim; to put it in terms of the form of a maxim that is *not* legislative, a maxim can *conflict* with the law iff the maxim *presupposes* the material object of the will, so that the object, not the law, determines the maxim (KpV 5:27).

In conclusion, the will plays a role in the causal origin of a *forbidden* action according to the moral law, since, according to Kant's causal theory of action, the concept of an action logically requires the will to play a role in the causal origin of the action and the causal law that connects the will and the action is the moral law. Since an action could not be forbidden unless the action conformed to Kant's causal theory of action, and since the causal connection between the will and the action is precisely the moral law, the moral law is a necessary condition of the possibility of its being forbidden, just as it is a necessary condition of the possibility of an action's being permitted. The other necessary condition of the possibility of an action is its maxim. Therefore, on Kant's causal theory of action, something is an action iff its moral determination is possible. Its *actual* moral determination, however, depends on the relation of its maxim to the moral law, and that depends on whether the maxim conflicts with the moral law or not, and that in turn depends on whether the form of the maxim is legislative or instead presupposes the (material) object of the will.

Only with *forbidden* actions, however, are we faced with the seeming paradox of how they result according to the very law that forbids them, but I hope that the air of paradox is now dispelled. The solution is, simply, that something is an action according to the moral law and according to its maxim, but an action is forbidden because of its maxim, which conflicts with the law. The distinction between the law and the maxim must be kept intact, as must the distinction between a causal law of freedom and a causal law of nature. With these distinctions, there should be no problem of the imputability of forbidden actions.

6 Maxims and Categorical Imperatives

6.1 The Possibility of Particular Categorical Imperatives

6.1.1 Two Apparent Problems with the Conclusion of the Last Chapter

The solution to the problem addressed in the last chapter creates an apparent problem of its own. The problem of the last chapter, i.e. the *new* problem of imputability, was the imputation to an agent of an action that violates the *causal* law that connects the agent and the action. The solution was that the causal law makes the connection regardless of whether the action violates the law or not. The action would be a violation because of its maxim, not because of its causal antecedents, i.e. the free will and the practical causal law; it is the maxim of the action that conflicts with or conforms to the law, not a causal determination of the will. A conflict or conformity is possible, it was argued, because the causal connection requires only the will's activation of the maxim according to the causal law, which makes the activation according to the law independent of the morality of the maxim. This leaves the maxim logically independent of the act of the will and of the law. This logical independence was characterized in the previous chapter as the maxim's being "end-loaded" onto the causation. Hence, the question of whether the maxim of an action conforms to the law or not is also logically independent of the law, and conversely, the law is logically independent of it.

A Humean or naturalistic type of causal connection between an agent and an action, on the other hand, reverses the relation of the maxim to the agent and her causal connection to an action. On this type of causal connection, the "*incentives*" that constitute the maxim (as Kant's use of the German word "*Triebfedern*" is translated into English in the Anglophone Kant literature) are *antecedent causal* conditions that are "front-loaded" onto the causal connection, but Kantians maintain it is paramount to point out that there is the crucial proviso that the maxim is *freely chosen* by the agent. Accordingly, maxims are not, contrary to the view put forward here, *consequent logical* conditions of an action that are "end-loaded" onto the causal connection, conditions that thereby only *identify* the action, but do not causally motivate it, and are constituents of actions whose *causal* determinations are completely independent of the maxims. On this partially naturalistic near universal interpretation among Kant scholars of the practical causal connection between the will and an action, the maxim is a necessary *causal* determination of an action, but only to that extent is it a Humean, naturalistic, or, more generally, a sort of causal connection between the will and an action that would make it *compatible* with the deterministic causal laws of nature. It would be a more fully Humean naturalistic causal connection were it not for the crucial character of the choice of the maxim and the activation of the maxim by the will, an activation that thereby constitutes the action, a character of the choice and activation that is represented as Kantian *freedom* or *spontaneity*. On such an interpretation of Kant, however, once the freedom of choice is rendered doubtful by "hard incompatibilists" who cannot find sufficient evidence for it, a full-blown determinism ensues and with it the disappearance of moral responsibility.[1]

The apparent problem created by the solution to the new problem of imputability is due to the possibility that maxims can themselves be categorical imperatives, or moral laws. For if a maxim of an action is itself a categorical imperative, it would be an instance of, or conform to, the law that causally connects the will to an action, which would seem to keep it from being logically independent of the law. Hence, the possibility that a maxim can be a categorical imperative would seem to contradict our solution in the last chapter to the new problem of the imputability of actions to the will whose causal involvement in the actions is logically necessary to their existence, since the solution requires that maxims are logically independent of the act of the will and the law that causally connects it to an action.

Moreover, this apparent problem of maxims that are categorical imperatives creates another apparent problem that would naturally be addressed at the same time. I have presented a maxim of an action in the now routine way as "incorporating" (Allison's expression) what is now standardly translated as the *incentive* of the action (Kant's *Triebfeder*), but which in today's psychological vernacular might be better translated as the *instinct*, *drive*, or *motive* of the action. An incentive for Kant, moreover, consists of a feeling (*Gefühl*), and the latter can originate with an inclination, desire, passion, and the various conditions of the will that Kant considers *external* to the will, are "pathological" (KpV 5:19), and get attached to the will only *contingently* (KpV 5:25, 26, 28), and thus get separated from conditions that Kant considers *internal* to the will and thus belong to it *necessarily*, viz., those that originate in *pure* practical reason—reason that is logically and causally independent of sense and sensation, which in practical philosophy for Kant devolves onto the feelings of pleasure and pain. The *further* apparent problem created is, first, that maxims that are categorical imperatives

---

[1] See Derk Pereboom, "Why We Have No Free Will and Can Live Without It," in *Reason and Responsibility*, Joel Feinberg/Russ Shafer-Landau, eds. (Belmont: CA, Thompson/Wadworth Publisher, 2005/2008, Thirteenth edition) pp. 464–77.

6.1 The Possibility of Particular Categorical Imperatives — 83

cannot contain, or incorporate, incentives that causally originate in inclination or passion, or any of the other sources of incentives that are "pathological" conditions of the will, since the source of the incentive of specifically categorical imperatives is the practical causal law itself. However, and here is the *further* apparent problem, since for a maxim that is a categorical imperative the source of its incentive, which is respect for the law, is the practical causal law itself, the maxim, which logically depends on its incentive, apparently must itself also *logically* depend on the law, since *its* incentive *causally* depends on the law. Consequently, it would appear that a maxim that is a categorical imperative cannot be logically independent of the causal law that is necessary for it to be a maxim of an action, that is, if the maxim is to constitute an action of a will that is free (i.e. Kant's causal theory of action). This, too, would therefore seem to contradict our solution to the new problem of imputability of the last chapter, viz., that the maxim of an action is logically independent of the causal origins of the action but instead determines only the causal *consequent* of a practical causation, i.e. an action.

A single distinction solves the apparent contradictions of the solution to the new problem of imputability that we reached in the previous chapter; again, the first apparent contradiction being that a maxim that is a categorical imperative cannot be logically independent of the practical causal law, since it would conform to, or be an instance of, the law, and the second apparent contradiction being that a maxim cannot be logically independent of the law, since (logically) necessarily, it would contain an incentive, and since its incentive would causally depend on the practical causal law, if the maxim were a categorical imperative, it would again logically depend on the law. With respect to the solution to these apparent contradictions, the very statement of the second apparent contradiction, however, immediately suggests a way to eliminate both apparent contradictions together.

Obviously, a maxim can be *logically* independent of the law that its incentive *causally* depends on, even though the maxim *logically* depends on its incentive. Just as obviously, there is an ambiguity in the second clause of the sentence just written: it is *logically* necessary that a maxim has an incentive, but it is only *causally* necessary that it has the incentive that it has. In the context of a maxim's logical independence of an incentive and in the context of an incentive's logical independence of the source of the incentive, whether the moral law or inclination, both expressions, viz., "maxim" and "incentive," have the implicit form of "maxim *in general*," or "maxim *as such*," and "incentive *in general*," or "incentive *as such*," leaving it an entirely *causal* matter regarding which incentives belong to which maxims. The same distinction between such a use of an expression involving "in general," or "as such," and a specific or particular use of the expression, that is, a use of the expression without the accompanying caveat of reference to the *concept* that is employed through the use of the expression, also dissolves the other apparent problem we are considering. Again, "maxim" is used as "maxim in general," or "maxim as such," and it is therefore independent of whether a maxim is a categorical imperative or not; accordingly, it is logically independent of whether it conforms to the Categorical Imperative in any of its three formulations, or not. Hence, it is logically independent of the causal law that results in an action, a conclusion of the previous chapter whose validity now seems untroubled by our concern about an apparent contradiction.

In summary, whereas every maxim is logically independent of the causal efficacy of the agent plus the causal law that leads to the action, not every maxim is also causally independent in the same way, since maxims that are categorical imperatives are causally *dependent* on the causal law in which the respect for the law that is the incentive of such maxims causally originates. This difference marks a fundamental distinction between the two sets of maxims: those that do (because of their incentives), i.e. categorical imperatives, and the incentives of those that do not (again because of *their* incentives), causally originate in the law that causally connects the agent and her action. So, while all maxims are logically independent of the causal law that leads to their actions, *only* maxims that are *not* categorical imperatives are *also causally independent* of the causal law that leads to their actions; *their* causal origins reside instead in inclination and passion, which produce "pathological" conditions of the will. Respect for the moral law is not "pathological."

6.1.2 Maxims can be Categorical Imperatives

The apparent problem presented by maxims that are not categorical imperatives cannot be solved by the claim that maxims cannot be categorical imperatives in the first place. Such a claim has been made in an attempt to solve the *old* imputability problem. Henry Allison disputed Lewis White Beck's interpretation of Kant's ethical theory that moral maxims, such as the requirement to be honest, are themselves categorical imperatives.[2] Allison argues that the distinction be-

---

[2] Lewis White Beck, *A Commentary on Kant's Critique of Practical Reason* (Chicago: University of Chicago Press, 1960), pp. 81–2. Henry Allison, *Kant's Theory of Freedom* (Cambridge, UK, Cambridge University Press, 1990), pp. 88–9. Previously, Bruce Aune had made an objection to Beck's interpretation (that maxims can be categorical imperatives) that, like Allison's objection, claimed that maxims were of the "wrong form" to be categorical imperatives. However, where "form" for Allision consists of a distinction between first- and second-order rules, Aune's con-

tween the Categorical Imperative in its three formulations and particular moral injunctions, such as the one commanding honesty, is a distinction between second- and first-order rules, and that Kant reserves the term "Categorical Imperative" for the second-order rules alone. But this for Allison is to override the very substantial amount of evidence of Kantian texts adduced by Beck and even added to by Allison without offering any reason for doing so other than Allison's assurance that his knowledge of what Kant actually meant is more reliable than Kant's own words on the subject: "Nevertheless, all of this [textual evidence] tends to obscure the *actual* relationship between maxims and objective practical principles that is operative in Kant's thought [*emphasis added*]."³ This issue would be no more than a "verbal problem" or "choice of mere words," i.e. whether or not to call first-order propositions that are maxims "categorical imperatives," were it not for the important distinctions that have been drawn just above that reflect a basic distinction between maxims that are categorical imperatives and maxims that are not—a distinction that itself is based on the causal, i.e. non-logical, relation between maxims whose incentives causally depend on the moral law, i.e. those that are categorical imperatives, and those whose incentives causally depend on inclination, i.e. those that are not categorical imperatives. Allison's position on this issue also makes a solution to another problem in interpretation of Kant's ethical theory impossible to solve in the way proposed in the next part of this chapter, viz., the problem of the presumed omission of a substantive step in Kant's derivation of the first formulation of the Categorical Imperative in the *Groundwork of the Metaphysics of Morals*—a problem and its solution that, again, will be addressed in the next part of the chapter.

Besides the evidence that Beck adduces for his interpretation and Allison in what can be considered a "good faith" "full disclosure," even adds to despite the fact that it counts against his own interpretation, there is the analogy between the relation between the three formulations of the Categorical Imperative and particular moral injunctions—themselves, Beck maintains, particular categorical imperatives—on the one hand, and the Principle of the Objectivity of Succession that headlines the Second Analogy of Experience, which is *a priori*, and "special," or "particular," empirical natural laws (*Besondere Gesetze*, KrV B 165))

---

sists of a distinction between particular propositions—particular categorical imperatives, such as the command to be honest—and their *generalization*, which is not a distinction between first- and second-order propositions. Aune goes on to claim that whereas categorical imperatives may indeed conform to the Categorical Imperative as Kant formulates it as three at least syntactically different propositions, their *generalization may not so conform*. See Bruce Aune, *Kant's Theory of Morals* (Princeton, NJ: Princeton University Press, 1979) p. 89.

3 Allison, *Kant's Theory of Freedom*, p. 88.

that empirically instantiate or exemplify the Principle, on the other hand. It is just an analogy, and it is weakened by the difference that not only are the formulations of the Categorical Imperative *a priori*, but so are the particular moral injunctions that conform to it, whereas only the general law of causality that is the Principle of the Objectivity of Succession is *a priori*, obviously, not the special empirical laws that conform to it.

Since it is Beck's interpretation that creates the apparent problem for our solution to the *new* problem of imputability, that would seem to argue in favor of Allison's interpretation, which does not create the problem, even though Allison's interpretation does create yet a further problem, the one mentioned just above, which I said would be addressed later in the chapter. But Beck's interpretation seems the right one, especially on both the strength of the textual evidence and its comfortable fit with the rest of Kant's theory, and since eventually there is a solution to the problem that it creates, where only Beck's interpretation also contributes to the solution of the further problem, a problem whose solution is made impossible on Allison's interpretation, Beck's interpretation will be the one that is adopted here.

6.2 Maxims, Categorical Imperatives, and a Presumed Omission in Kant's Derivation of the First Formulation of the Categorical Imperative

6.2.1 A Presumed Omission in Kant's Derivation of the Universalizability Formula of the Categorical Imperative

The fact that maxims can be categorical imperatives in Kant's theory provides a key to a resolution of a serious difficulty Kant scholars claim to have found in Kant's derivation of the first formulation of the Categorical Imperative—the so-called Universalizability Formula. Consequently, critics of Kant's such as Allison who insists that maxims cannot be categorical imperatives are depriving themselves of an available solution to the problem that they have tried to solve independently of the proposition that maxims can indeed be categorical imperatives.

The problem is brought to our attention once again by a recent book on Kant's theory of practical knowledge by Stephen Engstrom.[4] It begins with a reference to a presumed "slide" in Kant's derivation of the formula of universaliz-

---

[4] Stephen Engstrom, *The Form of Practical Knowledge: A Study of the Categorical Imperative* (Cambridge, MA: Harvard University Press, 2009), p. 5.

ability as it appears in the *Groundwork of the Metaphysics of Morals*.[5] Since the formula is here considered a *requirement* of practical reason of a maxim, it will henceforth be abbreviated as "UR."

UR: Act only on that maxim through which you can at the same time will that it become a universal law (G 4:421).[6]

In this respect, Engstrom's book continues a line of criticism begun by Bruce Aune in his book on Kant's moral theory,[7] subsequently pursued by Allen W. Wood in his book on Hegel's ethical thought[8] and in his first book on Kant's ethical thought,[9] and, for our purposes, concluding penultimately with Henry E. Allison's treatment of the perceived gap.[10]

The criticism of all four can be stated as follows: From the incontrovertible proposition that practical reason requires of a maxim that it *conform* to a universal law *in general* (*überhaupt*) (henceforth called the "conformity requirement" and abbreviated as "CR"),

CR: That a maxim conform to a universal law in general (G 4:421)

Kant derives the purportedly stronger proposition that practical reason requires of a maxim that it can be *willed* as a law for all rational beings, i.e. UR, the *volitional* requirement. That is, Kant derives UR from grounds that support only CR. Wood in particular has claimed that CR ought to be supplemented with the autonomy and humanity formulas of the Categorical Imperative for UR to be derived validly.[11] He has illustrated the weakness of CR with the counter-example of a rational egoist who could agree to CR but refuse to agree to UR, thus invalidating Kant's derivation of the requirement. The counter-example was subsequently cited by both Allison[12] and Engstrom.[13] Since CR is taken to be too

---

5 Engstrom, *The Form of Practical Knowledge*, p. 5.
6 Translated by Allen W. Wood, *Kant's Ethical Thought* (Cambridge, UK and New York: Cambridge University Press, 1999), p. 17.
7 Aune, *Kant's Theory of Morals*, pp. 28 ff.
8 Allen W. Wood, *Hegel's Ethical Thought* (Cambridge, UK and New York: Cambridge University Press, 1992) pp. 121–2.
9 Allen W. Wood, *Kant's Ethical Thought* (Cambridge, UK and New York: Cambridge University Press, 1999), pp. 81 ff.
10 Henry E. Allison, "On a Presumed Gap in the Derivation of Kant's Categorical Imperative," in Henry E. Allison, *Idealism and Freedom: Essays on Kant's Theoretical and Practical Philosophy* (Cambridge, UK and New York: Cambridge University Press, 1996), pp. 143–54; cited by Stephen Engstrom, *loc. cit.*
11 Allen W. Wood, *Kant's Ethical Thought*, pp. 81 ff.
12 Allison, *Idealism and Freedom*, pp. 146–7.

weak to entail UR, either the argument's validity depends on additional premises or the argument is simply invalid. Whereas Aune, Allison, and Wood declare the argument invalid as it stands, with Allison's attempting to make up for it with additional premises drawn specifically from Kant's *Critique of Practical Reason* as developed in his interpretation of Kant's theory of freedom and Wood's relying on the second and third formulations of the Categorical Imperative, Engstrom uses what he terms the "slide" to launch his book on Kant's theory of practical knowledge. There Engstrom claims to provide an understanding of Kant's theory that makes the derivation of UR defensible in terms of Kant's understanding of the notion of practical reason.

The two main theses of this part of the chapter are, first, that the appearance of such a "slide" in the *Groundwork*, as Engstrom characterizes the movement of Kant's thought, or a "gap," as, first, Aune, and then, Allison put it, or as simply a "fallacy," as Wood describes it, is *illusory*, and second, that the illusion is due to a failure to see how UR is in fact a valid conclusion from Kant's analysis of his concept of a categorical imperative that precedes the requirement. The discussion of the analysis that follows is intended to dispel the illusion. It will be argued that once the illusion is removed, the derivation of UR can be seen as a completed valid argument, without the need of any additional substantive premise to make its validity explicit, such as are offered by Engstrom, Allison, and Wood, but nonetheless acknowledging and allowing two presumably unexceptionable *principles of inference* as necessary to the derivation. As for Aune's, Wood's, and Allison's declaration that the argument is invalid as it stands, our discussion of Kant's analysis that dispels the illusion serves as a rebuttal of their view.

6.2.2 Hegel and the Traditional Criticism of the Derivation

Our four critics' objection to Kant's derivation of the volitional requirement actually amounts to a *defense* of the requirement against a traditional criticism of it begun by Hegel. This tradition has faulted the requirement *itself* as being useless in identifying moral maxims. The requirement is said to be so insubstantial that any maxim can qualify as moral. By pushing back the charge of insubstantiality from the volitional requirement itself onto its *derivation*, and in particular, onto the conformity requirement, our four critics indirectly confer on the volitional requirement the very substantiality that *both* creates the gap they

---

13 Engstrom, *The Form of Practical Knowledge*, p. 6.

claim to find in its derivation *and* rebuts the *traditional* criticism that it is the volitional requirement that is too insubstantial to identify moral maxims.

Thomas E. Hill, Jr. has staked out a position that falls between that of our four critics and Hegel.[14] Hill agrees with our critics that the derivation is faulty, but he also argues, now apparently in disagreement with them and in accord with Hegel, that UR *can* be read as a valid conclusion from CR, which would make UR, also, too insubstantial to identify moral maxims, and hence, for Hill, determine moral conduct. Hill maintains, however, that Kant "thought" that UR actually contains the substantiality in question.[15] Hence, UR can also be given the stronger reading. So Hill criticizes UR on two grounds: it allows, confusingly, both a stronger and a weaker reading *and* the stronger does not follow from the grounds offered in its support. Since this part of the chapter addresses the arguments of our four critics, it also addresses Hill's second criticism. But since we are not here dealing with the question of whether UR is actually substantial or not, and Hill seems more concerned with that issue, our attention will remain focused on just the four critics and only on Hill to the extent that he agrees with them on that issue.

Finally, this part of the chapter will only note the difference between the traditional criticism and the more recent one concerning the appearance of an omission in the derivation of UR, and it will do so without commenting further on the difference. Nonetheless, given the thesis that UR does indeed follow from CR, for the sake of argument it must be maintained that CR is just as substantial as UR, whatever degree of substantiality that may be. In any case, the argument of this part of the chapter will side with our critics in their dispute with the traditional criticism regarding the substantiality of UR in order to stay focused on our critics' claim that there is an omission in Kant's derivation of UR. But, again, this is done only for the sake of argument; this part of the chapter does not present its own case for the substantiality of UR.[16]

6.2.3 The Validity of the Derivation

In his analysis of his notion of a categorical imperative in the *Groundwork* Kant first states that every such imperative contains a law, i.e. a rule whose necessity

---

14 Thomas E. Hill, "Kant's Argument for the Rationality of Moral Conduct," in Thomas E. Hill, *Dignity and Practical Reason in Kant's Moral Theory* (Ithaca, NY: Cornell University Press, 1993), pp. 121–2.
15 Hill, "Kant's Argument for the Rationality of Moral Conduct," pp. 121–2.
16 I say more on this issue in 7. below.

holds *unconditionally*, that is, without the necessity's being relative to a condition that determines the rule, as is the case of the necessity that belongs to a hypothetical imperative (G 4:420 – 1). In the discussion that precedes the derivation of the Imperative, Kant ascribes this property (i.e. unconditionality) to a law (G 4:420). For example, the law requiring honesty is contained in a categorical imperative that acts as a constraint on one's will to indulge one's inclination to be dishonest, but that unlike a hypothetical imperative, it does not require honesty because, say, being dishonest eventually hurts one's business. Second, a categorical imperative requires of a maxim the necessity that it must *conform* to the law that is contained in the imperative (G 4:421). Third, the requirement of *unconditionality* entails that the maxim conform to the *universality* of law *in general* (*überhaupt*), since its unconditionality entails that there is no condition that can limit the *scope*, or *extent*, of the law (G 4:421). Kant then sums up the requirements of a categorical imperative with the statement that "this conformity alone [i.e. the conformity to the universality of a law in general] is what the imperative properly represents as necessary."[17] Since a maxim that conforms to the universality of a law in general *is* a law, or since only a law can be such a maxim that conforms to the universality of a law in general, or, again, since only a law conforms to the universality of a law in general, a maxim that *conforms* to the universality of a law in general *is* a law, the foregoing answers the question of how a maxim can be a law, and since a law has the property of universality, due to its subordination to a law in general, the foregoing answers the question of how a maxim can be a universal law. Each step advances a maxim from its start as a representation that *contains* a law (G 4:420), if it itself is a categorical imperative, or, equivalently, if it is a substitution instance of the universalizability *formula* UR of the Categorical Imperative, i.e. a formula of a universal law in general, to the stage at which it *is* a universal law. It all comes out of Kant's concept of a law and the requirement of practical reason of a maxim that it conform to a universal law in general.

The first part of this chapter is crucial to the conclusion that has just been derived, viz., that the maxim in question, to wit, a maxim that is a categorical imperative, is a law. For unless a maxim can be a categorical imperative, it would be invalid in the argument just concluded to conclude that the maxim in question is a law, since its being such an imperative is a necessary premise of the argument. That is why in the first part of the chapter I said that the dispute between Allison and Beck over the question of whether a maxim could be a categorical imperative

---

[17] Translated by Mary Gregor, Kant, *Groundwork of the Metaphysics of Morals* (Cambridge, UK: Cambridge University Press, 1997) p. 31.

6.2 Maxims, Categorical Imperatives, and a Presumed Omission — 91

is substantive and not merely verbal, with respect to the use of the term "categorical imperative." And that is why I faulted Allison's rejection of Beck's interpretation on more than textual grounds; there is the additional ground that Allison was depriving himself of the availability of a solution to the problem of the presumed omission in Kant's derivation of the Categorical Imperative.

The final question is how a maxim can be *willed* as a universal law. It seems an apparently uncontroversial, if not analytic, "principle of volition" that one can *will* what one's will, or practical reason, requires of one's maxim. It is the principle that the concept of an agent's acting on her maxim consists in her willing its object. A maxim is the principle on which the agent acts (G 4:421n). Since she acts by means of her will, for her to act is for her to will, and therefore for her to act on her maxim is for her to will its object. Therefore, if the *object* of her will is the very *maxim* on which she acts (G 4:447) and that it be a universal law, the act of her will would be *her willing that her maxim be a universal law*. Thus, the will would act on a maxim whose object would be the maxim itself, and the action would be that the maxim is a universal law. This should help clarify the terms in which UR is formulated and provide grounds for the principle of volition itself. In so doing, it should help explain why the principle of volition adds nothing substantive to the argument beyond the concept of *acting on a maxim by means of the will* and, also, *taking the maxim on which one acts to be its own object*. This analysis, of course, immediately aligns the first formulation of the Categorical Imperative with the third formulation, the principle of autonomy, since in identifying the object of the maxim with the maxim itself as a universal law, it identifies the action of the will with a universal law, and the act of the will would be the willing the maxim to be that law. It therefore would lend credence to Wood's contention that the derivation of the first formulation of the Categorical Imperative depends for its validity on the third formulation were it not for the fact that the analysis just given also supports just as well my contention that the derivation is complete as it stands, without the dependence on the third formulation, despite the fact that it is logically related to it, a relation Kant himself considers to be that of identity, which it should be noted, is not dependence between the identical items. I am arguing that the analysis on which the principle of volition rests is simply an application of the concept of a *willing* of the object of a maxim, and hence the object of an action, to the case in which the maxim is its own object, and it is willed to be a universal law, which is precisely what is required by CR, but required by CR without the explicit employment of the concept of willing the object of a maxim, as is required by UR. If the analysis is correct, it was simply a misunderstanding of this concept on Aune's part that brought about his search for the justification of the feature of UR that he apparently mistakenly thought was not already contained in the propositions leading up to UR, viz., the feature of willing a maxim as a universal law that was substantially different from conforming a maxim to a universal law in general. My claim is that the requirement to *conform* a maxim in a certain way just *is* the requirement to *will* the maxim in that way. After all, it is not peculiar to the requirement of UR that the maxim of an action is the object of the requirement; indeed, the requirement CR also takes the maxim of an action to be the object of the requirement, when it requires *of the maxim* that it conform to a universal law in general. With this analysis in hand, we can proceed with our use of the principle of volition. Henceforth, it will be used as a principle of inference in the derivation of UR and designated as "PV."

PV: One can *will* what one's will, or practical reason, requires of one's maxim.

Since one's maxim contains the "relevant" determination of the will, it contains that which practical reason requires of itself as so determined. In explanation of "relevant," a maxim of the will contains the determination of the will to take the very action in question. If it is practical reason that requires the determination, it seems evident that it cannot require of itself anything it cannot will. So, if practical reason requires something of its maxim, it can will what is required.

Armed with PV, we can deliver the answer to the question of how a maxim can be *willed* as a universal law. By the just adopted principle PV, if practical reason requires of a maxim that it conform to a universal law *in general*, one can *will* that it *conform* to a universal law *in general*. Since Kant's analysis of his concept of a categorical imperative shows that if a maxim *conforms* to a universal law in general, it *is* a universal law, it follows that if practical reason requires of one's maxim that it *conform* to a universal law in general, one can *will* that it *is* a universal law. In other words, since a maxim's *conforming* to a universal law in general entails its *being* a universal law, practical reason's requiring the former of one's maxim entails that one can *will* the latter. In short, CR entails UR.

The crux of the argument lies within Kant's analysis of his notion of a categorical imperative, and within that, his concept of a law. The crux is Kant's *subordination* of a maxim to a law in general. First, conformity of a maxim to a law in general subordinates the former to the latter. Second, since a law is an instance of a law in general, by the constraint of transitivity on the relation of subordination that is operative in our argument,[18] a law in general subordinates a maxim that conforms to the law in general. Therefore, a maxim that *conforms* to a law

---

18 Thanks to Sidney Axinn for his observation as a commentator on my paper containing these ideas at the Eastern Meeting of the American Philosophical Association, 2011, that mere subordination is not specific enough to justify my use of transitivity; hence I needed to add that transitivity is a *constraint*, or a *restriction*, on the relation of subordination in the present context.

in general *is* a law, since, more generally, a rule that is subordinate to a law in general is a law. In other words, the maxim itself becomes a law, for it is now, as subordinate to a law in general, an instance of a law in general. Indeed, this is exactly the result that Allison claims would be necessary, if the derivation of the volitional requirement were valid.[19] In short, the maxim becomes an instance of a law in general and thus itself becomes a law merely by conforming to the law that is contained in the imperative. *Indeed, this law—the one contained in the imperative –can be none other than the maxim itself!* Otherwise we get an endless series of ever more general laws that subordinate preceding laws without ever reaching a law *in general* or the Categorical Imperative itself, either of which can bring the series to an end, a regress that would be the bane of Kant's theory. To stop the regress in its tracks, Kant needs only the maxim, or the particular law, and the practical law in general, or the Categorical Imperative, to which the maxim conforms and through its conformity becomes a law.

To summarize the disillusion of an omission in Kant's derivation of the Categorical Imperative, the apparently uncontroversial PV plus the constraint of transitivity on the logical relation of subordination—our *other* principle of inference— have been employed to derive UR from a starting point that Kant's critics agree upon, namely, CR. From this minimal and apparently uncontroversial starting point we have been able to derive UR by employing both PV and the transitivity of subordination of a rule to a law, which, it has been argued, are contained in Kant's own analysis of his concept of a categorical imperative.

6.2.4 The Origin of the Illusion

It might be objected that this defense of the derivation of UR falls short of what I promised. The critics contend that a maxim's or an action's conformity to a universal law in general fails to tell us the difference on which is based the distinction between a moral maxim and action and an immoral one, whereas the possibility that a maxim or action can be willed as a universal law *can* tell us the difference on which the distinction between morality and immorality is based, since it can help the agent "decide" what to do—it is, as Aune argues, *a practical difference*[20]— whereas conformity to a universal law in general does not have such "practical import." I have argued, on the contrary, that UR is no stronger than CR, and hence that if UR can distinguish moral maxims from the rest

---

19 Allison, *Idealism and Freedom*, p. 149.
20 Aune, *Kant's Theory of Morals*, pp. 29–30.

such that an agent can "decide" which maxims are moral, which immoral, so can CR, and indeed that UR cannot make that distinction unless CR can make it: it distinguishes moral maxims from immoral ones on the ground that only the moral ones are universal laws, conforming as they do to universal laws in general. To sum up Aune's "practical import" difference, it seems to rely on a subjective phenomenon belonging to critics who followed Aune in finding the volitional requirement more useful in discriminating among maxims than the "conformity requirement." But though one may be more subjectively useful than the other, the now argued conclusion entails that there is nothing objective about the greater utility of the volitional requirement. Whereas to sum up my position, if a maxim conforms to a universal law in general, it *is* a universal law, and if it conflicts with a universal law in general, it is *not* a universal law.[21] So, contrary to what Aune and the critics contend, the condition of being a universal law distinguishes moral maxims from immoral ones, and the condition is satisfied iff a maxim conforms to a universal law in general, and finally, the formula that states the condition is the Categorical Imperative. Since this all seems so straightforward, it is a puzzlement how so many otherwise subtle and perceptive scholars of Kant's ethics seem to have overlooked the distinction or so misunderstood Kant so fundamentally.

By most accounts, as with mine, it started with Bruce Aune, who supported the idea of the omission on the basis of his claim that the principle on which UR rests, which I have formulated as CR and he designates as "L"

> "[L] is a higher-order principle telling us to conform to certain lower-order laws. But if we do not know what these lower-order laws are, we shall not find L a very useful principle. [UR] does not seem to possess this limitation. Even if I do not know what principles are properly considered universal laws, I know they are practical principles that, being universal, are binding on all rational beings. Knowing just this much, I could no doubt decide whether I could will that the maxims of many possible actions should be (or become) such laws. If, respecting a maxim *m*, I could not will such a thing, [UR] would show me that I ought not to act on that maxim, or that doing so is morally forbidden."[22]

As I read the text, however, Aune and I diverge from the very start. Our divergence turns on our respective readings of the principle from which Kant derives UR. Whereas I take it to be CR, Aune takes to be "Conform your actions to uni-

---

21 In fairness to Aune, he, too, recognizes this equivalence in Kant's theory, but since in his view conformity to universal law in general has no "practical import" that can help the agent decide what to do, CR still falls short of UR, despite the equivalence, *Kant's Theory of Morals*, pp. 30–1.
22 Aune, *Kant's Theory of Morals*, p. 30.

versal law" and designates as "L."²³ On Aune's understanding of the principle in question, the principle, or L, ends up being of no use at all, if we do not already know "what these lower-order laws are." On my understanding of CR, however, it instructs the agent to conform her actions, and thus her maxims, to a universal law *in general*, which I understand to be a *higher-order* law than the actions, and hence higher than the maxims, and therefore higher than the laws that are subordinate to it. Indeed, the principle would be the Categorical Imperative, or the moral law, itself, if being able to will one's maxim as a universal law, were included in the maxim, which I have argued can be so included on the basis of PV, provided of course that the maxim is a categorical imperative. It should be noted, moreover, that Aune, like all those who followed him in this connection, is quite aware of the expression of a generality, viz. the expression "in general," or *"überhaupt"* in the German, which I for one, but not, apparently, the others, understand for Kant to be logically independent of the particulars that fall under it, and hence not to be a generalization or an abstraction from the particulars, which they seem to take it to be. This basic divergence between Aune and me on the question of whether a maxim is to conform to a higher- or a lower-order law has the consequence that only on my reading of the principle on which UR rests, i.e. only on my understanding of CR, does the principle tell us which maxims are moral laws and which are not, for all and only such maxims that *are* laws are subordinate to, or conform to, the *higher-order* law. That is the import of my claim above that "a maxim's *conforming* to a universal law in general entails its *being* a universal law." Their understanding of the principle in question, on the other hand, does not include that entailment. From CR as I understand it I need only PV and the constraint of transitivity on the subordination relation to claim that CR entails UR.

Henry Allison explicitly accepts Aune's reading of the principle from which UR is derived, i.e. Aune's L, and not my understanding of CR. Allison asserts, "... the requirement 'Conform your actions to universal law as such [i.e. in general, or *"überhaupt"*]'. . . is practically uninformative; it does not provide any useful information about what one ought to do or ought not to do."²⁴ But on my understanding of CR, it does provide such information, since a condition that determines whether a maxim is a law or not does provide that information, and CR is that condition. Like Aune, Allison seems to take Kant to be imagining universal laws as given to an agent and generalizing that they conform to a universal law in general, whereas I take Kant to be imagining maxims as chosen, adopted,

---

23 Aune, *Kant's Theory of Morals*, p. 29.
24 Allison, *Kant's Theory of Freedom*, p. 145,

or even given to an agent and testing them for their conformity to a universal law in general, which is known independently of its instances. The purported instances pass iff they are universal laws. This alone, not Aune's method, explains the ease with which Kant derives UR from CR.

Allen Wood also accepts Aune's reading of the principle from which UR is derived, i.e. Aune's L, and not my CR.

> "Once again this tells no more than that our maxims ought to conform to whatever universal laws that there are. It does not tell us how to discover these laws and it does not entail that maxims conform to the laws whenever they pass the tests provided for in [the Universalizaibility formula of the Categorical Imperative and its involvement of the universal law of nature]."[25]

Like Aune's, Wood's interpretation of "a universal law in general" is "whatever universal laws that there are," which refers unhelpfully to particular universal laws, "whatever" they are, instead of my understanding of Kant's use of "in general" or "*überhaupt*" in CR, which refers to a higher-order independent condition that distinguishes maxims that are universal laws from those that are not. Consequently, Wood, like Aune and Allison, needs a condition that distinguishes maxims that are laws from maxims that are not laws, whereas I, having already located it in CR, do not need it.

Finally, in the following passage, Engstrom also accepts Aune's understanding of Kant's expression, "conform to a universal law in general." He says that Kant appears to

> "slide *from* the principle that a rational being should conform its will to any universal law it can recognize as valid for it as such [i.e. as valid for it as a rational being] (where this recognition is informed by its knowledge that what any such law prescribes as rational for one such being it must prescribe as rational for any other comparably situated) *to* the substantive and questionable principle that such a being should act only on maxims it can will as laws holding universally, for all rational beings."[26]

This is Aune's understanding of the principle (his L and my CR) from which UR is derived, since it requires only that a rational agent adopt a maxim or take an action that conforms to a universal law (Engstrom takes the agent as recognizing the law, whereas Aune leaves any particular law undetermined). But conformity to a universal law, while a consequence of rationality, is not an independent condition that only moral maxims or actions can satisfy and thereby distinguishes between the

---

25 Wood, *Kant's Ethical Thought*, p. 81.
26 Engstrom, *The Form of Practical Knowledge*, p. 5.

two sets of practical propositions. On my understanding of the principle, i.e. CR, however, the maxim, and hence the action, is to be, colloquially, "*measured against*," or according to, a universal law in general, which on my understanding is such an independent condition, and if the maxim or action satisfies the condition, or the test, it is a particular universal law. Hence, yet again, on my understanding of CR, that a maxim conforms to a universal law in general entails that it is a particular universal law. From there, since a maxim that passes the test is a universal law, it is a short step via PV plus the constraint of transitivity on the relation of subordination to *willing* that the maxim be a universal law.

6.2.5 Wood's Rational Egoist Objection

The rational egoist objection introduced by Wood fares no better. If the rebuttal against that objection is successful, the conclusion must be that since there can be no universal law to which a maxim determined by rational egoism must conform, the failure to identify a moral maxim laid at the feet of the conformity requirement actually lies not with the requirement, but with the assumption that rational egoism can provide such a law. The apparent triviality and thus helplessness as a guide to discriminating among maxims as moral or not of the conformity requirement and the ostensibly greater substantiality of the volitional requirement to be able to actually carry out the demarcation seem again to be due more to subjective factors than logical ones.

The objection, again, is that the egoist would be rational in recognizing the conformity requirement, but her rationality and her egoism would only be further enhanced if she were to balk at acceding to the volitional requirement, since her own objectives would only be thwarted, if not made impossible, if her maxim were indeed carried out universally. The last thing a rational egoist wants is for everyone's maxim to be like her own!

But this is the exact *opposite* of what a counter-example to Kant's derivation of the volitional requirement must be like. Since rational egoism determines that corresponding maxims cannot be willed as universal laws, and since it has now been argued that Kant's analysis of a categorical imperative entails that a maxim that *conforms* to a universal law *can* be *willed* as a universal law, it follows that practical reason cannot require of an egoistic maxim that it even *conform* to a universal law. The reason is simply that a rule determined by rational egoism is, well, *egoistic*, i.e. subjectively, and thus *not* objectively, *universal*, and hence, even if egoism is universal, its universality cannot be necessary with respect to the requirement of practical reason that a maxim conform to a law. If practical reason can require of a maxim that it conform to a rule determined by egoism, the rule can be no stronger than what Kant calls a "precept," or a hypothetical imperative, which may *in fact*, or *contingently*, be universal, but cannot be *necessarily* so, and hence cannot be a law according to which practical reason can determine a maxim. What may be necessarily universal, and thus a law that determines objects unconditionally in *theoretical* knowledge, or in nature, as may be the case with psychological laws determined by rational egoism, may be only contingently universal, and thus not a law at all, in determining the will unconditionally in *practical* knowledge. Therefore, a maxim determined by rational egoism cannot be a counter-example to Kant's derivation of the volitional requirement. Though everyone may be a rational egoist as a matter of human nature, it is impossible that the conformity requirement is satisfied by a maxim that is made by anyone on that basis.

It should now be evident that any maxim appearing as a counter-example to Kant's derivation of the volitional requirement must fail. Any maxim that cannot be *willed* as a universal law cannot *conform* to a universal law, and since any putative counter-example could not be *willed* as a universal law, yet *ex hypothesi* would *conform* to a universal law, nothing could actually be a counter-example that would demonstrate a gap or even a slide in Kant's derivation of the volitional requirement.

6.2.6 Conclusion

Though this part of the chapter has not addressed the traditional question of the effectiveness of the categorical imperative in identifying moral maxims, siding with the four critics of both Kant and of the traditional criticism for the sake of argument, it has attempted to rebut the objection of the four critics, that the derivation of the volitional requirement contains the slide or a gap introduced into the literature by Aune. Kant's notion of law and his constraint of transitivity of subordination relation have been the basis of the rebuttal.

7 Necessity and Practical *A Priori* Knowledge: Kant and Kripke

> "a law that is *subjectively necessary* (as a law of nature) is *objectively* a very contingent practical principle that can and must be very different in different subjects" (KpV 5:27)

7.1 The *A Priori* Knowledge and Necessary Truth of Categorical Imperatives

Having claimed to have restored completeness to Kant's derivation of the first formulation of the Categorical Imperative, we seem not to be faced with the question of its necessary truth, its seeming completely *a priori* derivation presumably being sufficient to establish the necessity of its truth. Kant is famous for seeming to hold that *a priori* knowledge can be knowledge of only necessary truth and conversely, necessary truth can be known only *a priori*. But analytic philosophy was confronted recently with a challenge to this view of a logical connection between necessary truth and *a priori* knowledge thereof, not just in the mind of Kant, but in the minds of analytic philosophers generally at the time who held to the tenet that the only philosophically defensible notion of necessity, if any such notion besides that of logic was defensible in the first place, lay in the rules that governed the use of our concepts and language. A notion of necessity pertaining to a reality that was independent of such rules was deemed incomprehensible, that is, *inconceivable*. Of the leaders in this shift in analytical thinking about the matter Saul Kripke and Hilary Putnam played the most prominent roles.[1]

But having just attempted to provide fresh ground to Kant's claim to have derived the universalizability formulation of the Categorical Imperative without committing the error of omission, we must face the challenge mounted, now especially by Kripke against Kant, albeit in a somewhat different context—the difference of which will actually be the very theme of our argument—that the *a priori* nature of our knowledge of categorical imperatives is necessary to the necessity of their truth. To that challenge we now turn our attention.

---

[1] Saul Kripke, *Naming and Necessity* (Cambridge, MA: Harvard University Press, 1980, originally published 1972), p. 35, 159, and Hilary Putnam, "It Ain't Necessarily So," *Journal of Philosophy* 59 (1962), pp. 658–671, also in his *Philosophical Papers volume 1* (Cambridge, UK: Cambridge University Press, 1975). See also Putnam's, "Explanation and Reference" in his *Philosophical Papers 2*

7.2 Kripke's Complaint About Kant

Saul Kripke complains that it is wrong for Kant to hold that every statement whose truth is necessary is known *a priori*, and also wrong to hold, conversely, that every statement whose truth is known *a priori* is necessary. For Kripke, there are certain necessary truths that are known *a posteriori*, and there are certain truths that are known *a priori* that are contingent.[2] In this chapter, I am not going to take issue with Kripke's complaint just as it stands, but will explore its *conjunction* with his response to a certain question that he asks. It is the question, with respect to the truth of a given statement, whether "it might have been otherwise." In apposition, he asks, "Is it possible that, in this respect, the world should have been different from the way that it is?" He then asserts that this is a question about "a fact about the world." He continues, "If the answer is 'no,' then this fact about the world is a necessary one. If the answer is 'yes,' then this fact about the world is a contingent one." In sum, whether it might have been otherwise that a given statement is true, that is, whether its truth is necessary or contingent, it is Kripke's contention that the question "in and of itself has nothing to do with anyone's knowledge of anything."[3] Since Kripke recognizes that the notion of aprioricity belongs to epistemology, his assertion that his question has "nothing to do with anyone's knowledge of anything" agrees exactly with what I am calling his *complaint* about Kant, viz., that Kant fails to recognize necessary truths that are known *a posteriori* and also, truths that are known *a priori* that are contingent.[4]

Everything I have just reviewed about the conjunction of Kripke's complaint about Kant and his assertion about the distinctness between necessity and knowledge can be given a weaker and a stronger interpretation. A weaker interpretation focuses on just the *distinctness* between the two alethic modalities and knowledge, and thus at least allows consideration of what Kripke calls a "substantive philosophical thesis," viz., that the modalities depend on the knowledge.[5] This interpretation would emphasize the expression "in and of itself" as it qualifies the question being asked. If the distinction between necessity/contingency and knowledge is all that Kripke is insisting on, then a philosopher such as myself could try to persuade Kripke of Kant's "substantive philosophical thesis" that in certain cases the modalities do indeed depend on knowledge, or at least that necessity depends on *a priori* knowledge.

---

[2] Saul Kripke, *Naming and Necessity.*
[3] Kripke, *Naming and Necessity*, p. 36.
[4] Kripke, *Naming and Necessity*, p. 35.
[5] See Kripke, *Naming and Necessity*, p. 36.

The other, stronger interpretation of what I have reviewed about Kripke is to downplay the expression "in and of itself" and instead maintain that Kripke actually argues *against* the substantive thesis that necessity and contingency depend on knowledge. On the stronger interpretation, Kripke's assertion that they have "nothing to do with knowledge" would by a certain line of argument keep them from depending on knowledge in *any* case in which Kant, for one, alleges the dependence. It will be seen at the end of our discussion of Kripke that if we were to adopt this stronger interpretation, we would have to conclude that Kripke must reject the particular dependence of necessity on *a priori* knowledge that I ascribed to Kant in the previous chapters and that I will continue to do so in the present one. Since the *ipsimma verba* of *Naming and Necessity* seems to favor the weaker interpretation—after all, Kripke does say "in and of itself"— its adoption is not only a more textually secure path to follow, but it allows us to leave it open to Kripke to adopt the substantive thesis, which I think most would agree can fairly be attributed to Kant.

Now, Kripke's complaint about Kant makes it clear that he rejects Kant's *universal* thesis that *every* necessary truth depends on our *a priori* knowledge of something. And I said initially that I am *not* going to take issue with Kripke's rejection of this thesis of Kant's. But this diffidence does not extend to yet *another* question, one the I *will* ask, and it will occupy us for the remainder of our discussion of Kripke. It is the question of what would be Kripke's position regarding Kant's substantive thesis about just *certain* statements whose truth Kant takes to be necessary and whose necessity he claims depends on our *a priori* knowledge of their truth? Are there *some* truths that must be known *a priori*, if they are to be necessary, as Kant alleges? And could Kripke agree with Kant that there are such truths, and if so, could he agree with Kant on the particular statements—for Kant, truths—that we have already considered as categorical imperatives, including such as the prohibitions against lying and breaking one's promise?

7.3 The Target Statement of Kripke's Complaint about Kant

The statements cited by Kripke whose necessary truths can be known *a posteriori* or whose *a priori* knowledge is contingent all belong to the knowledge that Kant calls *theoretical*. This suggests that statements that for our purposes support Kant's substantive thesis about the dependence of the necessary truth of just *certain* statements on our *a priori* knowledge of them lie outside theoretical knowledge. Since Kant divides knowledge between the theoretical and the practical, the necessary truths we are looking for that support Kant will occur in practical knowledge, if they occur at all (KpV 5:43).

The line of argument adopted in this chapter of the book, therefore, does not follow one rather recent defense of Kant against Kripke with regard to natural necessity. I will not be interpreting Kant's conception of natural kinds and natural necessity generally as an alternative to Kripke's conception, including the latter's understanding of the fact that the atomic number of gold is 79, or even that "gold is necessarily a yellow metal."[6] Rather, I will be taking a different tack entirely, by looking to practical knowledge instead of theoretical knowledge to find a response to Kripke on Kant's behalf.

The tack I adopt is based on the following strategy. As I have already employed several of Quine's theories in the Preface and in 1., I will do so again in this instance. He has argued that it is only under an initially specified condition that a necessary ascription of a property to an object can be made determinate, or unambiguous. That is, he maintains that an object must be taken to be subject to an initial condition that is independently taken to stand in a necessary relation to a given property, if the property is to be said to be necessary with respect to the object. Otherwise, the property would be ascribed to the object unconditionally—in what Quine calls an "extensional" and therefore referentially "transparent" statement—thereby rendering the ascription empirical, and hence, contingent. The contingency would thus conflict with the supposed necessity of the ascription, and there would be no way to resolve the conflict, since it would originate in the ambiguity of the two types of reference involved, one, that would be transparent (and hence, the contingency of the truth of the statement) and the other, opaque (and hence, the necessity of the truth of the statement). The trouble for Quine with adopting this sort of argument for the sake of the possibility of a necessary ascription of a property to an object is that if the enabling condition is taken to be a condition of the *existence* of the object that is independent of our reference to it and not a condition of merely the *reference*—taken ontologically and not logically—Aristotelian essentialism would be reintroduced into metaphysics, to Quine's and many other philosophers' horror, Saul Kripke's and the recent spate of doctrines of metaphysical realism having done so notwithstanding. Quine has recourse to a way of resisting the perennial temptations of speculative metaphysics—however much based, for example, on Kripke's latter day theory of the use of ordinary names of objects and properties. Quine's recourse is to banish attempted necessary ascriptions of properties to objects altogether. This would eliminate the alethic modalities

---

[6] For this sort of response to Kripke's complaint about Kant regarding Kant's theory of necessity see Robert Hanna, "Why Gold is Necessarily a Yellow Metal," in *Kantian Review*, vol. 4 (2000), and his *Kant and the Foundations of Analytic Philosophy* (Oxford University Press, 2001), chs. 2,3, and 5.

from our philosophical logic at their root and enable ontology to proceed without their induced unresolvable ambiguities of reference.

Kant avoids the pitfalls of speculative metaphysics of concern to Quine by accepting the logic of his argument, but rendering the condition that supposedly has a necessary relation to the property that can only now be necessarily ascribed to the object merely a condition of reference, not a condition of the object's independent existence. Quine's distinction between the two types of condition, again, is that a condition of reference blocks substitution of identities of reference, thereby keeping it from being a condition of the object's independent existence; it is a condition that induces what Quine calls an "opacity," in contrast to a transparency, of reference. The latter alone pertains to the object as it exists independently of any reference of ours to it. It will be along such a line as this that our response to Kripke on Kant's behalf will provide not just Kripke with an opportunity to consider it a "substantive metaphysical thesis," but us, too, with an opportunity to explain what is meant by claiming eponymously that our choices of maxims constitute the "bounds of freedom" beyond which the idea of free will loses its meaning.

7.4 Kant's Shift from Theoretical to Practical Knowledge[7]

Kant shifts the objects under discussion from theoretical to practical knowledge. The former includes the objects with which Kripke is concerned: objects that are *given* to us. For Kant, objects are given to us through intuition, either *a priori*, which occurs through synthesis of the understanding in intuition, as in mathematics, or *a posteriori* through empirical intuition that is distinct from synthesis, as the given in science and in experience generally.

Objects of *practical knowledge* for Kant, however, are objects of the will, not intuition, and need only be represented instead of being given in intuition (KpV 5:9n, 15, 21, and 23 ff.). The will is our power to bring these objects into existence through our actions (KpV 5:9n). I have asserted throughout the preceding discussions that the existence of the actions consists in part in the will's enactments of the maxims chosen by the agent. In sum, objects of practical propositions for Kant involve actions of the will that are chosen by the agent through her maxims, not objects upon whose existence our intuitions of them depend, but objects that

---

[7] 7.5.–7.9. agree at many points with *A Commentary On Kant's Critique of Practical Reason* by Lewis White Beck, especially pp. 70–102, although there are many points at which there is a lack of agreement, if not a divergence, as well.

are brought into existence through actions that we bring about by means of our will. Whereas a sensible *intuition* of an object depends on the object's existence, the existence of the object of an action of a *maxim* depends on the *maxim's* being chosen by the agent and its being willed.

So, the argument that follows is that Kripke's complaint about Kant applies to Kant's account of *theoretical* knowledge, but not to his account of practical knowledge, with the objects of our knowledge shifting accordingly, from being objects of intuition that are given to us to being objects of the actions of our maxims that are chosen by us; in the case of our intuitions of the objects, the intuitions depend on the existence of the objects, whereas in the case of the objects of actions of our maxims, the maxims, and hence the actions, are chosen, and the existence of the actions—the enactment of the maxims—and hence the existence of the objects of our actions, depends on our will. In sum, Kripke's complaint about Kant omits Kant's notion of practical necessity, which provides a way for Kripke to reconsider his view that what he considers the highest degree of necessity of the truth of a statement might be a property of a practical proposition *that must be known in order to be true.*

* * *

So far, our discussion has primarily focused on the causal relation between the will and the action of a maxim. But it has not done so to the exclusion of the *non-causal* relations between either the will and an action or, to a lesser extent, an action and its object, i.e. the object of the will (see 3.2.–4., especially 3.4.). Our present discussion of Kant's notion of a necessity that depends on our knowledge of it, however, requires that our primary focus now shift to the relation between an action and its object—a means-ends relation— and in particular the means-ends relation in which the end is not logically connected to the means, i.e. the action. A major difference between the discussions of the two chapters is that 3. was concerned with the subjectivity of the empirical, and hence contingent, conditions of the agent's will, and thus the subjectivity of the *maxims* of her actions, whereas in this chapter we are primarily concerned with the subjectivity of the empirical, and hence contingent, relation of a *precept*, or a certain type of means-ends relation, between an action and its object. Consequently, if the means-ends relation is empirical, and hence for Kant contingent, it is preceptive, and therefore if it is not preceptive, and thus is not contingent, and therefore not empirical, it is *a priori* and *pure*, that is, it is devoid of pleasure and pain. Consequently, the mean-ends relation would in that case be objective and the action, moral. It would be a relation between an action's being right and its being good.

7.5 The Unsuitability of Happiness as a Universal Principle of Action

Kant holds that *by nature* every human being desires only his or her own happiness. But he avers that despite its being the sole universal practical principle of human nature, happiness is too general a notion to prescribe (*vorscheiben*) by itself any specific action, since any specific object that is desired for the sake of happiness will vary from person to person and vary even for the same person over time, since desires are based on expectations of pleasure from the objects that are desired, and they, varying as they do from person to person, or for a given person over time, ultimately determine only what Kant calls "practical subjectivity" (KpV 5:25).[8] That is, since actions vary according to the desired objects, they, like the objects they actualize, will vary according to the pleasure one takes in the objects, and again, the pleasure varies from person to person. Hence, if happiness is the principle of action, nothing universal can be prescribed with respect to any *specific* action that is necessary to bring about a desired object. Consequently, for any individual, happiness is a principle of action that if *not* supplemented by representations of objects that are agreeable or pleasurable for the individual, leaves *undetermined* a specific object of desire, and hence fails to prescribe a specific action that is necessary for bringing about such an object (KpV 5:20, 25). In other words, the necessity is blocked by the variability. On the other hand, if the principle of happiness *is* supplemented by reference to the pleasure a person takes in an object, the supplementation keeps the original notion of happiness from *directly* serving as a universal principle of action. Therefore, the sole universal principle of human nature with regard to desire—happiness—leaves it to another faculty of mind to provide a universal principle that *can* sufficiently determine the faculty of desire that a specific action is thereby determined. For Kant, there is such a faculty and it is the faculty of practical reason (KpV 5:31, *et passim*). It alone, Kant maintains, and not the desire for happiness, can determine a specific object of the faculty of desire that it is possible that a specific action that can actualize the object can thereby be determined.

---

[8] For the sake of simplicity and convenience, among the feelings we get by means of sense, henceforth reference will be made only to happiness consisting of pleasure or agreeableness and not the absence of pain or disagreeableness. In other words, pain and aversion are omitted from the present account.

7.6 The Unsuitability of a Precept as a Practical Law (*praktische Gesetz*)

Reason, however, can still be of *indirect* service to a person who desires happiness, as based on expectation of what is agreeable or pleasurable for the person. Since every precept of an action is a rule of reason that falls under the general determination that is contained in a basic practical proposition (*praktische Grundsätze*), the rule is the constituent of the proposition through which reason determines the action that is necessary, if the desired object is to exist (KpV 5:20). This entails that a person's inclinations that are included in what I will henceforth call the *context of the precept* are part of the determination of an action required for the achievement of a specified object. A context of a precept thus essentially involves the particular subject, the objects of whose representations would be brought about only through action. So, which object it is among the many that might contribute to a person's happiness must await the specification of the object by the individual according to the rule that is to be followed, as based on the individual's expectation of pleasure from the object in the context of the precept, if any action is to be prescribed by the rule as being necessary to the person's enjoyment of the object. Consequently, in such a case, the truth of a basic practical proposition whose subordinate rule prescribes the action will be *practically contingent* upon the individual's specification of the object according to these just mentioned factors in the context of the precept, based on the person's expectation of getting pleasure from the object. That is, in such a case, the practical proposition about a specific object and its necessary action *could be false*, since its truth varies from person to person according to the context of the precept. The possibility of falsehood entails that there is the possibility that for different individuals or for the same individual in a different context of a precept a different object might be the specified, or desired, object, and therefore an action originally prescribed might not be prescribed.

Kant denominates as "practical precepts," "i.e. hypothetical imperatives" (KpV 5:20), the rules of practical reason that, as subsumptions that fall under the general determinations that are contained in basic practical propositions, prescribe actions under these empirical, and hence for Kant, *contingent* conditions that belong to the respective contexts of the precepts (KpV 5:20). They prescribe specific actions as necessary for the satisfactions of antecedent determinations of desires for specific objects. But it is only as necessary in that respect that such actions are required. Their necessity is thus hypothetical, or conditional, upon the individual's specification of the object, which in turn is conditional upon these other variable factors that shape one's pursuit of happiness. Since the condition, or contingency, upon which they depend is the individual's respective specifications of the objects desired, as based on the expected pleasures from the objects in the respective contexts of the precepts, the necessity is characterized by Kant as *subjective* (KpV 5:20). Consequently, such *subjective necessity* is for Kant a practical *contingency*, and is the same *practical subjectivity* that was introduced just above as the reason for the unsuitability of *happiness* as a universal principle of action. The truth of a practical proposition that is thus characterized as *subjectively necessary* is therefore only *practically contingent:* though the proposition is true in an actual context of a precept, or in Kripke's semantics, true at the actual world, it is not true in every practically possible context of the precept, or at every possible world. The alternative possible contexts have just been generally described in our discussion of the variability inherent in the precept of an action that would be required for the achievement of an object of desire, which itself must await the individual's determination in every practical context of the precept.

7.7 Subjective Necessity as Both Practical Contingency and Natural Necessity

Since the object of one's desire for happiness must await the individual's specification, if the basic practical proposition is to be complete, it is only through reference to an individual's specification of such an object that the practical knowledge or proposition expressing such knowledge can be characterized as one whose truth is *subjectively* necessary. These very facts, however, can be known only in *theoretical* knowledge, where the necessary truths are not subjective, but objective judgments—the understanding's use of concepts. As theoretical knowledge, their necessity will partake of the *a priori* condition that determines all possible (Kantian) appearances with respect to the logical functions of judgment—the objective unity of self-consciousness that depends on the use of the categories, which are logically necessary to natural law in general (*überhaupt*) (B 165). When it comes to nature, the truths of judgments about the necessary temporal order of the occurrences of appearances according to the specific category of causality, in respect of natural causal law, are objectively necessary (B161–63). That is, the truths about such ordered appearances are objectively necessary—the appearances must occur in the order in which they do occur, since the order is determined according to the category of causality and the category is an *a priori* mode of knowledge. The appearances partake of the necessity that belongs to the *a priori* concept (the category) of which they are instances. That is a statement of Kant's determinism of nature. Natural determinism applied to theoretical knowledge of an individual's specification of an object of desire entails that the specification is determined by natural law. Therefore, the subjective necessity of a precept that relates an action to its desired object, i.e. a hypothetical imperative, is both theoretically necessary and practically contingent.

Finally, relative to practical knowledge, contingency is a property of truths of basic practical propositions that conform to precepts, due to their dependence on any individual's specification of an object of desire in the context of the precept. But relative to theoretical knowledge, a judgment about the relation between a specified object of desire and its context of precept is necessary without qualification, since theoretical knowledge views the specification as the natural causal consequence of the factors that belong to the context of the precept, and thus as conforming to natural law, and thus eventually as turning on the feeling of pleasure the individual expects from the objects desired. Desire based on such feeling is determined by psychological laws, which are natural, and, of course, involve necessity, even though the particular feelings belonging to particular psychological judgments make those judgments theoretically contingent. This psychological necessity, however, cannot be part of my argument that certain necessities depend on just certain *a priori* knowledge, since I effectively waived recourse to it when I decided to look outside theoretical knowledge for the dependence in order to provide a response to Kripke's complaint about Kant.

Kant, in effect, antipodally anticipates Quine's naturalization of epistemology,[9] by epistemologizing nature, where the sensible conditions of knowledge are understood by Kant as limitations on the object that is known, such that it is unknown insofar as it is unconditioned—Kant's transcendental idealism. Whatever Kripke's understanding of natural law might turn out to be, that is, whether or not it is an instance of Kripke's necessity, he is definitely right that Kant epistemologizes nature: for Kant, truths that are naturally necessary are relative to any sensible conditions of knowledge. And these are among the truths that appear in theoretical knowledge.

7.8 Practical Laws and Precepts

In Kant's defense, his characterization of the truths of basic practical propositions that are precepts for actions as necessary to the achievement or existence of their objects as merely practically subjectively necessary, as equivalent to instances of natural laws, and finally, as merely *practically contingent* indicates that he recognizes the limitations of these practical subjective necessities relative to possibilities that belong to practical knowledge as distinct from theoretical

---

[9] W. V. O. Quine, *Ontological Relativity and Other Essays* (New York and London: Columbia University Press, 1969), ch. 3.

7.8 Practical Laws and Precepts

knowledge. Basic practical propositions that are true in every possible context of a precept, and thus hold for every possible subject, i.e. rational being, or closer to Kripke's terms, at every practically possible world, and hence are practically objectively necessary, are independent of these sensible limitations of theoretical knowledge. As we discussed at length in the previous chapter, Kant calls these propositions *practical laws* and the necessity of their corresponding rules is *unconditional* (KpV 5:20).

Unconditionally necessary practical rules for Kant are independent of the contexts of the precepts that render the necessity of precepts subjective. They alone are practically *objectively* necessary. First, they are independent of every individual's own specification of an object of desire, and accordingly, are independent of the context of the precept of the action. Consequently, they cannot be determined by what Kant calls a *material object* that is the end of an action prescribed by a practical rule of reason whose necessity is conditional (KpV 5:21). They thus must conform to the form of law, which Kant considers the objective necessity of a rule of reason (KpV 5:27). Absent any prior material object, the content of a proposition whose necessity is unconditional must first be determined only by the form of law. Objects thus become determinable by the form of law with respect to the necessity that belongs to laws.

Precepts of actions as necessary for actualizing the objects of the actions, and thus of the will, are introduced into our discussion as standing between the practical causal *laws* that causally connect the will to the actions and the *maxims* of the actions, maxims that *in general* do not have the practical necessity that belongs to rules of practical reason, both laws and maxims that have been discussed in previous chapters (though, as we have found in 6.1.–2.), *certain* maxims *can* be practical laws). Whereas the rules of practical reason whose necessity is unconditional are practical *laws* and the *maxims* of actions in general do not have the practical necessity that belongs to rules of practical reason, the rules of practical reason that are necessary but whose necessity is conditional are rules of practical *precepts*.

Since on Kant's causal theory of action—the main thesis of this book— the agent's will is logically required to play a role in the causal origin of her action, but since the necessity of the precept of her action with respect to its object is conditional, if the practical relation between her will and its object is based solely on the precept of her action, it cannot be lawful, and thus cannot be causal, and hence her will cannot play a role in any practical causal origin of the object, assuming the transitivity of causal laws and hence causal dependencies, and also assuming Kant's principle that efficient causality entails causal law between antecedent and consequent.

In summary, there can be no practically possible world at which a basic practical proposition that is a law, and hence on Kant's causal theory of action is a causal law, is false. Any practically possible world at which a basic practical proposition is false must be a world in which, prior to the determination of an action, an individual first specifies her own object of desire in a context of the precept of the action. Since every practical law is independent of every such prior determination of an object of a prescribed action, every practical law, and thus on Kant's causal theory of action, every practical causal law, is independent of every practically possible world at which it could otherwise be false, as Kripke would put it.

7.9 Kant's Practical Causal Laws as Kripke's Necessities

Kant's account of the necessity of natural laws, and thus the subjective necessity of the causality of a practical reason whose precepts are only conditionally necessary, cannot be our response to Kripke's complaint about Kant. Just as earlier I could not rely on the particular natural necessity that is psychological, I also effectively waived my recourse to the necessity of natural laws in general when I shifted our attention from theoretical to practical knowledge to make my response to Kripke.

But I have defended Kant against the *conjunction* of Kripke's complaint about Kant, that, contrary to Kant's position, some necessary truths are known *a posteriori* and some truths known *a priori* are contingent, *and* Kripke's thesis that "in and of itself" necessity and contingency have "nothing to do with anyone's knowledge of anything." Whereas I am not contesting the complaint itself, I am claiming that it is not true for Kant that all necessities are theoretical. Kripke's complaint is thus, for the sake of argument, allowed to apply to Kant's view of natural laws, which govern the subjective conditions that determine precepts of actions. But for Kant, there are also the necessities consisting of the conditions of a person's *practical a priori* knowledge of practical, or moral, law which, according to the thesis of this book, is practical causal law. Such law connects the will of the agent with her action through her *knowledge* of it (KpV 5:19), and it is independent of the very subjective conditions that keep a connection between the will and its object from being causal and instead make a prescriptive connection between the will and its object conditional. Just as Kripke uses necessity to relegate certain truths that are known *a priori* to contingency, so in the epigram at the top of this chapter, Kant uses practical objective necessity to relegate to practical contingency the subjective necessity that determines the context of the precept of an action according to natural law.

Identifying Kant's practical contingency with his natural necessity and his natural law by way of the subjective necessity of precepts for actions, and viewing his natural necessity and natural law as relative to human knowledge, and then allowing, again for the sake of argument, Kripke's thesis that certain *a priori* truths are only contingent, we can proceed by analogy: As Kripke has contingency stand to necessity, so Kant has practical contingency, that is, for him, theoretical necessity, stand to practical objective necessity. The analogy aligns Kant's practical contingency with Kripke's contingency and Kant's practical objective necessity, and thus his practical law, and hence, on his causal theory of action, his practical causal law, with Kripke's necessity. By analogy we can then attribute as high a degree of necessity to Kant's practical law, and thus his practical causal law, as Kripke ascribes to his necessity; in other words, we can ascribe the highest degree of necessity to Kant's practical law, and thus his practical causal law, even in Kripke's estimation of it, as we might imagine it to be.[10]

If this analogical reasoning is valid, the conjunction of Kripke's complaint about Kant with his view about the distinctness between necessity/contingency and knowledge can now be given either to two responses on Kant's behalf. On the stronger interpretation of Kripke's remark that necessity and contingency have "nothing to do with anyone's knowledge of anything," since for Kant a practical law's, and thus a practical causal law's, necessity holding for anyone depends on her knowledge of it, it would seem that Kripke could not agree with Kant about this.

On the weaker interpretation, however, if Kripke had considered Kant's practical philosophy he might not have come to such a dire conclusion concerning Kant's views about the relation of necessity to *a priori* knowledge. He might have seen the analogy between his necessity and Kant's practical objective necessity and acknowledged that the latter might indeed be a case of the former.

Whether we adopt the stronger or the weaker interpretation of Kripke's remark about the relation of necessity and contingency to knowledge, however, Kant's defense against Kripke's complaint could be that Kripke just failed to consider Kant's theory of *practical* knowledge. There Kant talks about practical reason, or the will, apart from any prior limitations of sense that would keep a basic practical proposition from being a law, and thus on my interpretation, a causal law, whose distinctness from sense is the only way we should consider a practical law, he claims, if we want to understand the possibility of our practical knowledge of truths that are necessary and whose necessity depends on our *a priori* knowledge of them.

---

10 Kripke, *Naming and Necessity*, pp. 99, 125, 164.

8 The Bounds of Freedom

8.1 Making Objects Actual

In 7.8. I argued that for Kant the will cannot make its object actual, if the means-end relation between its action and its object, that is, the object of its action, is a mere precept, since the necessity of a precept is conditional upon the empirical conditions and circumstances of the agent, including the agent's expectation of pleasure from her possession of the object and whatever empirical laws connect the empirical conditions and circumstance and the existence of the object. The necessity of a practical causal relation, on the other hand, is legislative, and hence, unconditional in the respects just mentioned, which it would be if the will were *practically (note bene: not theoretically)* causally responsible for the existence of its object, since efficient causal connections for Kant entail causal laws, whether the laws are practical or theoretical. Of course, this leaves open the possibility that the will *could* make its object actual, if the necessity of the relation between its action and its object were legislative, and hence unconditional, and on the interpretation of Kant's practical law offered here, viz., practical law as *causal* practical law, being legislative implies being *causally* legislative. Such would be a *practical* causal relation between the will and its object, or the object of its action—a relation according to the moral law, on the interpretation of the moral law argued for here. But, of course, such an object would not be a material object, and hence, not an empirical one. It would be what Kant considers good or evil, either of which would be ascriptive of the will, but neither of which would be understood hedonistically, or in terms of pleasure and pain.

The distinction between the two types of means-ends relation between an action of the will and its object—that is, the will's or the action's object—is the basis of Kant's distinction between two "forms" of maxim (KpV 5:27–30). One form constitutes the possibility just considered, viz., where the means-ends relation between an action and its object is unconditionally necessary, and hence, on the interpretation of Kant's practical causal law offered here, can be practically causally legislative; the other form constitutes the immediately preceding possibility, viz., where the maxim is not practically causally legislative, but where its object is *presupposed* by the maxim (instead of the object's causally depending on the action, and thus on the (free) will of the agent) (KpV 5:20ff., and 5:34). In case and only in case the relation is presupposition is the object a material, and hence empirical, object, which would therefore be hedonistically determined.

As I have drawn our attention previously to the parallel between empirical intuition and maxim for Kant (4.5.) the distinction between these two forms of maxim parallels the distinction between Kant's two types of relation between an empirical intuition and the intuited object. On the one hand, a causal law of freedom connects the causal efficacy of the intuited object (viewed as a thing in itself) with the appearance—the undetermined object of the empirical intuition. On the other hand, the intuition presupposes the appearance—a logical, not a causal, relation.

8.2 The Non-legislative Form of a Maxim Creates a Certain Problem for Our Interpretation of Kant's Moral Law

The non-legislative form of a maxim creates a problem for our interpretation of Kant's moral law as his practical causal law that is similar to the problem that we had to face in 5. regarding the possibility of the imputability of forbidden actions. There, the problem was that since I argued that Kant's practical causal law is his moral law, it was seen to be trivially true, yet seemingly paradoxical, that the will was said to be able to bring about a forbidden action only if the action, being forbidden, *violated* the law—something that would be incomprehensible if we are thinking of a causal law in the way that we think of a causal law between a cause and its effect as a natural law: no effect can possibly violate the very natural law that connects it to its cause.

The problem our interpretation of Kant's practical causal law as his moral law creates this time, however, is somewhat different from the problem of 5. Now, since on Kant's causal theory of action the moral law practically causally connects the will to its action, and since Kant asserts that the object of an action is made actual only through the existence of the action, then, if the relation between an action and its object is a mere precept and not a causal law, and thus the maxim of the action would be *non-legislative*, the will would be causally involved in practically bringing about the action without its being causally involved in bringing about its object. This is not to say, of course, that the will would not be involved at all in bringing about its object, for it would remain just as causally involved in the causal origin of its action as it would be if its maxim were legislative and if its precept just happened to result in the achievement of its material object, for the action, and hence the will, would indeed be involved in the achievement, only it would not be *causally* involved. Though the precept, and thus the will, would not be causally involved in the achievement, it would be going too far to say that it would not be involved at all in the achievement: when getting an assist from natural law, a prudent choice of precept can help achieve one's goal. In this instance, Hume would be right, that reason would be the "slave of passion," which is the role of reason in Kant's hypothetical imperative.

Our new problem is readily resolved, however, once it is seen that the existence of the action is only a *necessary* condition of the existence of its object, not a sufficient condition. Thus, the necessary condition might be satisfied, and still the object of the action might not be made actual. Indeed, that is Kant's point about a precept: it can prescribe an action without the implication that the object of the action would thereby be made actual. In a related manner, that is also his point that as the object of one's actions, happiness cannot specify an action that would bring about the happiness, since there can be no practical causal law for the action to bring happiness—the relation of the action to its object would be only a precept.

8.3 Action without Passion and Independent of Nature

Actual passion or sensation of pleasure or pain only accompanies action, but is not a causal consequence of it (according to practical causal law), though of course *representation* of passion can be part of a maxim, as we have been noting throughout. If a form of a maxim presupposes the material object of the will, or of the action, the presupposition might fail. Thus the exercise of the causal efficacy of the will with respect to the enactment of the non-legislative maxim might enact the maxim but not actualize the material object of its action. On the other hand, if the form of a maxim is legislative, the action might again exist independently of its material object, since the material object has already been abstracted from the maxim—the form of the maxim's being distinct from its matter, as Kant would put it (KpV 5:21). In either case, therefore, whether the maxim is legislative or non-legislative, the action might be brought into existence without the same thing happening to its material object. Passion for Kant, therefore, can only accompany action, but cannot be causally connected to it. Consequently, the causal efficacy of the freedom of the will cannot extend to the passions, or the sensations of pleasure and pain that constitute what Kant considers the material of a maxim.

The realm of passion—actual feeling—is thus one boundary beyond which freedom cannot travel with causal effectiveness. Another is the physical wherewithal without which a person cannot achieve the object of her will by means of bringing about the action that answers to her maxim (KpV 5:20 ff.) The causality of freedom cannot reach into and thereby affect nature, which is determined by physical, or more generally, natural laws. But both passion and nature are limitations on freedom only because they and freedom are both causally and logically independent of each other. There is a third realm, however, that is not causally independent of freedom and upon which freedom itself is logically dependent, and this is the realm of maxims whose enactments causally depend on freedom, but without whose enactments, and therefore without the maxims themselves, freedom could bring about nothing, that is, could have no effect whatsoever.

8.4 The Center of the Circle of Maxims

I have argued throughout the foregoing discussion, going all the way back to 2., that Grice's notion of ordinary causation and Kant's empirical or natural causation are logically and causally mutually independent of their respective notions of sense-data, appearances, and maxims that, *seriatem*, constitute perceptions of objects understood according to Grice's causal theory of perception, Kant's appearances of things that appear (which are definitely not his *things in themselves*), and his actions of the will understood according to his causal theory of action (3.). As the fundamental practical propositions that constitute references to actions so understood, maxims and their actions, understood as the objects of the maxims (see 5.4.), are causally and logically mutually independent of Kant's natural causations: natural causations have no entry into the circle of maxims. But, as I have just said, their enactments do causally depend on the freedom of the will and the freedom could have no possible effect were it not for the enactments, and therefore were it not for the maxims that get enacted. Thus do the boundaries of the causal efficacy of the freedom of the will shrink from the actual enjoyment of pleasure and the absence of pain to the physical capacity to achieve one's goals and now to the perimeter of the circle of maxims. But the bounds of freedom get even narrower than that.

Since maxims are freely chosen by the agent, the freedom of her will is limited by her power to freely choose her maxims (*frei Willkür*). But since her maxims are fundamental practical propositions that contain general determinations of her will, she can choose only maxims that contain general determinations of her will. These determinations, in turn, are limited by the very nature of a maxim in general, viz., a fundamental practical proposition that the subject regards as valid only for her will (KpV 5:19). Consequently, the agent can choose only among determinations through which she can empirically distinguish her will from the will of everyone else, since through these determinations of her will alone can she view her maxims as valid only for her will: "this necessity is conditioned only subjectively and *cannot* be presupposed to the same degree in all subjects" (KpV 5:20, italics added. See also KpV 5:20–1). But, apparently paradoxically, these determinations are none other than the very ones from which her will is *free* but that from a naturalistic point of view would be the *causal* determinations of her will. In other words, the boundaries of her freedom would have shrunk to the point that her will would have been reduced to that very point, around which the antithetical perimeter of the *causes* of her actions would now revolve, a point around which the former bounds of her freedom—her principles, or her maxims—would have been replaced by constraints that put her will in bondage—the very causal origins of her actions from which her freedom was supposed to have made her will an independent agency. One and the same point—her will—would have become the center of two antithetical boundaries, one the center of freedom in the practical causal origin of action and the other the center of bondage in the theoretical-natural causal origin of action,[1] the differences among which were adumbrated earlier in the book.[2] This point would thus be located at the center of Kant's transcendental idealism.

The will would be at the center of not just Kant's transcendental idealism, however, but also, and *therefore*, as well, at the center of my single object/dual aspect account of his causal theory of action that was described in 1.3., among other places. In playing a role in the causal origin of the empirical conditions belonging to the enactments of the maxims that constitute its actions, it creates the very bounds it cannot circumvent without making itself ineffective. The same causality of its freedom to enact its maxims in actions transforms the empirical conditions of its subjective constitution from the enclosures of the determinism of nature into the expanses of the freedom of action. Thus can only the will create its own liberation from its merely reacting to emotional bondage, by enacting maxims according to the practical causal law—the moral law—whether the maxims are in harmony with the law or not (see 5.4.).

8.5 The Last Word: The Incentive to be Moral

Finally, it might seem that the above interpretation of Kant's causal theory of action and his naturalistic account of the same commits him to the view that our will is in bondage to our inclinations, Kant's ubiquitous profession of the freedom of the will from our inclinations notwithstanding. But to draw this inference would be a mistake. It is true that I have said that for Kant the only maxims on which the subject acts are fundamental practical propositions she considers valid only for her will; and I have also said that the general determinations of her will that are contained in these maxims must therefore enable her to distinguish her will empirically from everyone else's will, which entails that the deter-

---

[1] For a closely related idea of antithetical philosophical arguments revolving around a mere vanishing point to which one side reduces the other, see Thomas Nagel, "Moral Luck," in *Mortal Questions* (Cambridge, UK: Cambridge University Press, 1979).
[2] See Division I, Section A and Division I, Section B, in 1.4. and developed further in 3.2.–3.

minations are empirical. Indeed, unless this were true, I could not also hold, as I clearly do hold, that these same determinations belong among the *causal* determinations of the will insofar as it plays its role in the causal origin of actions, (where, it should be remembered, the actions are definitely *not* understood according to Kant's causal theory of action, for in such a role the actions are not determined by any maxims). How, then, it is rhetorically asked, can the will be *causally* independent of these determinations, which it must be if it is to be free? Even if they are said to be "freely chosen," would not calling the choice "free" be merely a *façon de parler*? Would not Kant be simply trying to turn a necessity into a virtue by merely *embracing* the necessity and calling it a "free choice"? His so-called "libertarianism" would be sorely tried, if that were so.

My answer to the charge against what I have said, an answer that I have already referenced, in 3.2., consists in Kant's claims, first, that every maxim contains an incentive, but also, second, that an incentive can originate with practical reason itself. The answer to the charge, then, is that empirical determinations of the will are not restricted to inclinations, since incentives are such determinations and among them there are intellectual incentives that originate in pure practical reason. Since everyone has pure practical reason, everyone has in a given situation subject to moral judgment the incentive to do what is moral for its own sake—that is, do it for the sake of duty. So, the answer to the charge is that the agent distinguishes her will from that of everyone else on the basis of its "constitution," its "subjective conditions" (KpV 5:20–1), but among these there is always the incentive to do what is morally necessary for its own sake, and finally for this incentive to be the one that is contained in the maxim on which she *acts*, is for her to *choose* that maxim! It is as simple as that.

References

Allison, Henry E., *Kant's Theory of Freedom*. Cambridge, UK,/New York: Cambridge University Press, 1990.
—— "On a Presumed Gap in the Derivation of Kant's Categorical Imperative," in Henry E. Allison, *Idealism and Freedom: Essays on Kant's Theoretical and Practical Philosophy*.(Cambridge, UK and New York: Cambridge University Press, 1996.
Aune, Bruce, *Kant's Theory of Morals*. Princeton, NJ: Princeton University Press, 1979.
Ayer, A. J., "The Causal Theory of Perception," *Proceedings of the Aristotelian Society, Supplementary Volumes* LI, 1977.
Beck, Lewis White, *A Commentary on Kant's Critique of Practical Reason*. Chicago: University of Chicago Press, 1960.
Engstrom, Stephen, *The Form of Practical Knowledge: A Study of the Categorical Imperative*. Cambridge, Mass., Harvard University Press, 2009.
Greenberg, Robert, *Kant's Theory of A Priori Knowledge*. University Park, PA: Penn State Press, 2001.
—— *Real Existence, Ideal Necessity: Kant's Compromise*. Berlin and New York: Walter de Gruyter, 2008.
Grice, H. P., "The Causal Theory of Perception," in *Proceedings of the Aristotelian Society, Supplement*, vol. XXXV, 1961, reprinted in large part in *Knowledge: readings in contemporary epistemology*, ed. Sven Bernecker and Fred Dretske. Oxford: Oxford University Press, 2006.
Hanna, Robert, *Kant and the Foundations of Analytic Philosophy*. Oxford University Press, 2001.
—— "Why Gold is Necessarily a Yellow Metal," *Kantian Review*, vol. 4 2000.
Hill, Thomas E., "Kant's Argument for the Rationality of Moral Conduct," in Thomas E. Hill, *Dignity and Practical Reason in Kant's Moral Theory*. Ithaca, NY: Cornell University Press, 1993.
Hudson, Hud, *Kant's Compatibilism*. Ithaca and London: Cornell University Press, 1994.
Kant, Immanuel, All references are to the Akademie edition (Ak) of *Kants gessammelte Schriften*. Berlin: Walter de Gruyter, 1902. Specific references are to the *Groundwork of the Metaphysics of Morals* (G), the *Critique of Pure Reason* (KrV), following the standard notation of the A and B pagination of the first and second editions, the *Critique of Practical Reason* (KpV), the *Metaphysics of Morals* (MS), and *Religion Within the Bounds of Mere Reason* (R), and translations are either by various translators, including Werner Pluhar (KpV), Mary Gregor (G), Norman Kemp Smith (KrV), and Henry Allison and Paul Guyer (KrV), or myself.
Korsgaard, Christine, *Creating the Kingdom of Ends*. Cambridge, UK: Cambridge University Press, 1996.
Kripke, Saul, *Naming and Necessity*. Cambridge, MA: Harvard University Press, 1980, originally published 1972.
Nagel, Thomas, "Moral Luck," in *Mortal Questions*. Cambridge, UK: Cambridge University Press, 1979.
Pereboom, Derk, "Why We Have No Free Will and Can Live Without It," in *Reason and Responsibility*, Joel Feinberg/Russ Shafer-Landau, eds. Belmont: CA, Thompson/Wadworth Publisher, 2005/2008, Thirteenth edition

Price, H. H.. *Perception*. London: Methuen & Co. Ltd., 1954, first published, 1932.

Putnam, Hilary, "It Ain't Necessarily So," *Journal of Philosophy* vol. 59, 1962, also in his *Philosophical Papers volume 1*. Cambridge, UK: Cambridge University Press, 1975.

—— "Explanation and Reference," in G. Pearce and P. Maynard, eds. *Conceptual Change*. Dordrecht-Reidel, 1973, and in his *Philosophical Papers volume 2*.

Quine, W. V. O., *Word and Object*. Cambridge, Mass, New York and London: MIT Press and John Wiley & Sons, Inc., 1960.

—— "Epistemology Naturalized," in *Ontological Relativity and Other Essays*. New York, NY: Columbia University Press, 1969.

Reath, Andrews, *Agency and Autonomy: Kant's Moral Theory*. Oxford, UK, New York: Oxford University Press, 2006.

Sidgwick, Henry, "Appendix, The Kantian Conception of Free Will," in *The Methods of Ethics*, seventh edition. Indianapolis, IN: Hackett Publishing Company, Inc., 1981, first published 1907.

Strawson, P. F., *Individuals: An Essay in Descriptive Metaphysics*. Methuen & Co. Ltd., 1959.

—— "Perception and Its Objects," in G. F. Macdonald (ed.) *Perception and Identity*: Essays Presented to A. J. Ayer. London: Macmillan, 1979; reprinted in *Knowledge:* readings in contemporary epistemology, ed. Bernecker and Dretske.

—— "Causation in Perception," in *Freedom and Resentment and Other Essays* (Oxford/NewYork, Routledge, 2008, first published, Methuen & Co., 1974.

—— "Imagination and Perception," in *Freedom and Resentment*, first published in *Experience and Theory*, ed. Lawrence Foster and J. W. Swanson. Amherst, MA: University of Massachusetts Press, 1970.

Wood, Allen W., *Hegel's Ethical Thought*. Cambridge, UK and New York: Cambridge University Press, 1992.

—— *Kant's Ethical Thought*. Cambridge, UK: Cambridge University Press, 1999.

—— "Kant's Compatibilism," in *Self and Nature in Kant's Philosophy*," ed. Allen W. Wood. Ithaca and London: Cornell University Press, 1984.

Subject index

Actions 43, **61–80**, 82, **114–5**
– Actions and Events 8–13
– forbidden actions 57–60
Allison, Henry E. 48n, 52, 53n, 54, 63, 66, 68–70, 82, 84–86, 87–8, 90–1, 95
analytic philosophy XIX, 3–4, 13, 14–5, 74, 99
appearance [and event] 5–6
– appearances: Kantian concept of 8, 56, 74, 76, 108, 115
Aristotle 10, 13, 29, 102
ascription 19, 36, 52
Aune, Bruce 84n–85n, 87–88, 91–2, 93–6
– Kant's Theory of Morals 94
– autonomy 91
Ayer, A.J. 15–16, 20, 39n

Beck, Lewis White 84–86, 90–1, 103n
belief 68
bounds of freedom 103, **112**, 115–6
Britain 29

Categorical Imperative XIV-XV, XVII, XVIX, 1–7, 17, 56, 65, **81–98**, 99 [see also Kant: moral law]
Categories, applied to appearances 56, 107
causal concept[s] **5–6**, 17, 68
Causal Efficacy regarding the Maxim that constitutes its Action [CEMA] 61, 63, 64–5, 66
Causal Efficacy regarding the Sense-Data that constitute its Perception [CESDP] 41–2, 46
causal law 73, 80, 83–4, 112–3
causal origin 2–4, 7, 8, 36, 60, 80
causal relations 38–9, 112
causal theory 6, 8, 41–4, 63–65, 70, 72 [see Kant]
– **causal theories of objects** **14–40**
– causal theory of perception [see Grice]
causality **41–5, 57–58**
cause and effect 33, 35, 36, 61, 67–8, 73
compatibilism **49–51**, 75

Conformity Requirement [CR] 87–8, 89, 92, 93–97
Conscience **57–60**
consequences **31–9**
constraint 15, 48, 90, 92–3, 95, 97–8
contextualist 52
contingency 100–2, **107–108**, 110–11
continuant 39–40 [see also endurant]

data 18–19, 22, 37–39, 41, 46
Davidson, Donald 16n, 75, 76
desire 82, 107, 108
derivation **88–89**, 93, 98
description 10, 16–18, 30, 49, 53, 61
determinism 52, 73, 75, 76, 79, 82, 107–8, 116
direct reference 10, 12–13, 29–31
discrepancy 24–5, 36–7, 41, 61
dualism XVIII, 7–8, 38 [see ontology]

egoism **97–8**
Empfindung [sensation] 43
empiricism 5, 7, 61, 74, 79, 104, 112, 115
endurant 39–40 [see also continuant]
Engstrom, Stephen 53n, 86, 88
– *The Form of Practical Knowledge* 96
entailment 20, 48, 57, 62, 76, 95
epistemology 3, 100, 108
equivalence 94n, 108
essentialism 102
ethics 2, 4, 13, 62n, 68, 94
events [see also 'appearance'] 7, 8
existence 5–10, 14–8, 40, 55–6, 103–4, 112–4
experience 1, 16–17, 55
expression 8, 10–11, 13, 30–1, 83–4, 95–96
external object 9–12, 33–4, 43–53, 62

faith 85
free will 1–2, 3, 63–5, 69, 72, 77, 81

Subject index

freedom 1, 43, 63, 67, 68, 72–74, 78 **112–117**
– **freedom of will** XIV, 4, 5, 12, 13, **57**, 78–9, 115
Frege, Gottlob 30
front-loading 73–74

Gavagai 8, 13, 31n
Gefühl [feeling] 43, 82
generality 55 [see also quantification]
Gibbon, Edward 10, 13, 28–9
given object 9–10, 43
good 62, 64, 67
Grice H.P. 4, 9–10, 14–15, **17–33, 41–6**, **55–6**, 61, 115
– sense-data 15–16
– theory of perception 3, 22–23, 24–26, 31–33, 36–39, 40, 41–49, 54–55, 115

Hanna, Robert 102n
Handlung ['action'; see also will] 3
happiness 105, 106
Hegel, G. W. F. 87, **88–9**
Hill, Thomas E. 89
honesty 90
Hudson, Hud 74–77
– on Kant's compatibilism XIX, 75
human 68, 98, 105
Hume, David XVI, 8, 52, 61, 68, 81–2, 113

idealism 57
identity 8, 14n, 39–40, 56, 75, 91
illusion 88, **93**
immediacy 55
incentive 83, **116–7**
incompatibilism 46–9, 52, 82
independence 36, 81, 83, 114–5
individual 54–6, 105–10
imperceptibility of the agent 21–4
imperative 68
imputability 61–80, 81
incorporation thesis 54, 68
indeterminism 73, 74–6
instinct 82
intuition 73–4, 104

judgment XVI, XVIII, 2, 22–3, 54, 107–8

Kant, Immanuel XIII, XVI-VII, 1, 15, 41, 56
– causal concept 5–7, 55
– **causal law 65**, 70, **110–11**
– causal theory of action XX, 6, 12, 43–44, **46–49**, 49–60, 61–2, 80, 83, 109–110, 115–6
– causal theory of memory 59–60
– *Critique of Pure Reason* [Kritik der reinen Vernunft / KrV] XVIII, 1, 10, 57, 59, 66, 71, 85
– *Critique of Practical Reason* [Kritik der praktischen Vernunft / KpV] 47, 57, 58, 64, 65, 70, 71, 99, 105, 106–7, 109, 110, 112, 115, 117
– ethical theory 48, 94
– on freedom XIII, XVIII, 68, 74–5
– freedom of will 3, 6, 17, 55, **57–58**, 62–3, 64, 71, 75
– **& Grice 43–6**
– & Grice & Strawson 58–9
– *Groundwork of the Metaphysics of Morals* 65, 71, 85, 87, 88, 90, 91
– **incompatibilism 46–48**
– **& Kripke 99–111**
– maxims 47, 54, 55, 80
– metaethics 2, 3, 13
– **moral law** XVI, 47, **65–66**, 68, 70–1, 90, 98, 110, **113–114**
– **moral theory** XIV, XVII–XX, **1–4**, 5, 15, 62–3, 66, 87, 116
– moral thought 11, 62
– natural law 68
– noumenal causality XIII–XIV
– objective succession XVIII
– philosophical system 5, 111
– practical law 47, 61, 64, 109, 110–11, 112
– practical reason 47, 56, 82, 105, 106
– practical subjectivity 105
– *Religion within the Limits of Reason Alone* 54
– theory of action 4, 49–51, 55, 61, 105, 113
– **Theory of Practical Causality 41–56**
– transcendental freedom XIII–IV, XVI, 79
– transcendental idealism XIII, XVIII, 4, 7, 57, 108, 116
– universal thesis 101

Kantian Review 102n
Korsgaard, Christine 69–70, **78–9**
– *Creating the Kingdom of Ends* XIX
knowledge 99, 101, **103–104**
Kripke, Saul 10, 29, **99–111**
– *Naming and Necessity* 100, 101, 111

language 8, 30–1, 99
law 65, 109
Leibniz, Gottfried Wilhelm 52
liberation 116
libertarianism 117
Locke, John 14
logic XVI, 18, 31–33, 35, 36, 38, 83, 99, 103

material object 15, 80, 114
mathematics 103
maxims 81–98, 104
meaning 2, 7–8, 10, 30–1
Meerbote, Ralf 75, 77
memory 10, 13, 26–28, 31–1, 46, 59–60
metaphysics 4, 102, 103
mismatch 24–5, 41, 61
monism 75
modality 25, 41, 100–2
morality 62–3, 67, 116–7
moral law 65–6, 67–9, 78–9 [see also Kant]

Nagel, Thomas 116n
natural law XIII, XV–VI, 61, 64, 66, 69–70, 78–9, 107–8, 113
nature 72–74, 105, 108, **114–5**
necessity 99–111
necessities 110–111 [see also Kripke]
neutral 62–5, 67
normative law XIII, 63, 64
normative principle XIII

obligation 68
objects 8–9, **14–40**, 42–5, 98, 103–109, **112–3**, 115 [see also external]
omission 86–98, 99
ontology 7–**8, 36–9,** 102–3
opacity 103

pain 60, 112
perception 21–4 [see also Grice]
Pereboom, Derk 82n
philosophy 5, 22, 74, 100, 111
physical law 75, 114
pleasure 60, 82, 105, 115
possibility 32, 38, 40–3, **81–6**
practical law [praktische Gesetz] 64–5, 71 **106–7, 108–110**
precepts 108–110, 114
presupposition 114–5
Principle of Volition [PV] 92, 93, 95
Price, H. H. 45
principle 47, 71
Principle of the Objectivity of Succession 85–6
proposition [*Satz*] 71
Putnam, Hilary 99

quantification 37, 55
Quine, Williard van Orman 2, 7–8, 16n, 30–1, 63, 102–3, 108

rationalism 67, 74, 97–8
rational agency 52–54
realism 102
reason 1, 56, 57, 60, 106, 113, 117
relation 52, 55–8, 75, 85, 91, 103–4, 112–4
Reath, Andrews 53n, 54
reciprocity 1, 62
representation 56, 79, 90, 105–6, 114
Rome 13, 28–9

science 103
self-consciousness XVI, 107
semantics 107
sense-data 22, 24, 32, 33–34, 37–39 [see also Grice]
sensation 1–2, 14, 43, 57, 59–60, 79–80, 82–3, 114
sensibility XVIII, 2
Sidgwick, Henry 48, 62, 63–4, 67
society XX–XXI, 5
spontaneity 69, 82
Strawson 4, 9–10, 14, 15–17, 18, 20, 23n, 26, 39n, 41–2, 44n, 55, 59

subjective necessity 107, 110–11
subjectivity 45–6, 54–6, 104–5, 107
substitution 40, 103
synthesis 103

temporality 39, 58
theory of perception XIX, 3, 25 [see also Grice]
time 36–39, 55–6
transcendental freedom XIII, 79 [see Kant]
transparency 102–3
Triebfedern [incentives] 53–4, 81 truth 2, 100, 101, 104, 107–8
typology 11n, 59

unconditionality 51, 67, 90, 98, 102, 109, 112
understanding 3, 5–7, 103

universal law 90, 91–2, 94, 96, 97
Universal Principle 105, 107
Universalizability Formula 86–7, 90, 99
Universalizability Requirement [UR] 87, 88–9, 92, 93–96
utterance 30, 10–13
variability 51, 105, 107
vengeance 50–1

will XV–XVI, XVIII, **XX–XXII**, 5, 11–12, 43, 51, **57–8**, 61, 63, 65, 66, 70, 72, 75–76, 78, 81–2, 115–6
Wood, Allen W. XIII, 14, 53n, 57, 66–70, 87–8, 91, 96, **97–8**
– *Kant's Ethical Thought* 96

www.ingramcontent.com/pod-product-compliance
Lightning Source LLC
Chambersburg PA
CBHW030657230426
43665CB00011B/1129